Office Origami

The Highly Successful Slacker's Guide to
Workplace Procrastination

Office Origami

The Highly Successful Slacker's Guide to Workplace Procrastination

Adam Russ

Universe

First published in the United States of America in 2005
by UNIVERSE PUBLISHING
A division of Rizzoli International Publications, Inc.
300 Park Avenue South
New York, NY 10010
www.rizzoliusa.com

ISBN 0-7893-1313-8
Library of Congress Catalog Control Number 2005901714

2005 2006 2007 2008 / 10 9 8 7 6 5 4 3 2 1

Produced in 2005 by
PRC Publishing
The Chrysalis Building
Bramley Road, London W10 6SP
An imprint of Chrysalis Books Group plc

© 2005 PRC Publishing

Printed in Malaysia

Credits

Illustration and project selection by David Mitchell. Project introductions and ancillary words by Adam Russ.

Picture Acknowledgements

Origami photographs © Chrysalis Image Library / Simon Clay.
All further photographs obtained via stock.xchng, IV. We wish to thank the following contributors for allowing us to use their material: Rene
Meulenbroek [7629_4566], Annette Gulick [34904_2150], Brenton Nicholls [40613_1818], Mischar Jung [43433_5725], Lyndon M Smith [43609_5720],
Lucian Binder [52049_2715], Nick Cowie [84582_5476], David Stiller [95091_8352], Mark Hillman [136805_9242], Ijansempoi Ronen [157394_2585],
Armend (AD). M [163859_7507], Bryan Powell [168735_3145], Davide Guglielmo [205250_4029, 211248_2423, 211523_4106, 211550_4113].

All illustrations © Chrysalis Image Library / David Mitchell

Contents

The Path of Office Origami

Welcome to the inscrutable world of Office Origami, the lotus path to workplace serenity. If all around you co-workers are so stressed that clumps of their hair are falling out, be still. Within this book you will follow the path of corporate indolence, and rather than sneer at your lack of any discernible effort at your job, those around you will think you are really cool; for nothing impresses quite like origami made from the latest efficiency directive. While around you accounts are being won and lost, assets liquidized, and interest accrued, your concerns will transcend such worldly pettiness. Instead, you will learn to contemplate the last perfect fold in an index card that creates the flying dragon, and be at one with the universe.

Imagine the looks of wonder and admiration that you will receive in that vital board meeting when after fiddling in your lap for a few minutes you are able to produce a perfectly formed paper frog! And made from a business card no less. Imagine the delight on the faces of CEO and Chairman alike as that frog begins to jump its way around the table. Humdrum takeovers will soon be forgotten about, and your corner office on the top floor is assured.

The Path of Office Origami can also improve your romantic life. Picture the scene: you are at the water cooler; as usual the cup dispenser hasn't been refilled; and here comes a thirsty member of the opposite sex from the sales division you want to ask out (once you've worked out how to do that without breaking any sexual harrassment laws). As they bemoan the usual lack of paper cups, to their amazement you will be able to fashion one instantly from the contents of the nearest wastebasket, thus establishing yourself as interesting and resourceful. From there you're a short step away from being ravished in the photocopying room.

It can take a lifetime to fully appreciate the art of Office Origami, so do not rush yourself or allow wordly concerns—such as submitting an urgent report or paying attention in meetings—to come between you and enlightenment. There may be times when your serenity is threatened, for example it takes a master Origamist to ignore an incensed client screaming over the desk. Remember though, that client will easily be awed by a display of your powers. Weave a multimodule star before his eyes and watch his fury wilt. To ensure his complete submission, play the Elephant on a Motorbike practical joke on him—he will be putty in your hands. In fact there are very few difficult situations that cannot be resolved with Office Origami. Having said that, many of its followers have found that it has failed to prevent one from getting laid off. However, the Grand Masters of Office Origami are devoting themselves to this problem whenever they can be bothered.

This leads us to anti-origamists. There will inevitably be a few non-believers who interpret your papery spiritual journey as laziness. These people need your patience and tolerance. Gently explain that while you *could* be reconciling March's sales figures, Office Origami is a gentle activity that improves the environment, stimulates the brain, sharpens the concentration, steadies the emotions, and is proven to increase productivity by 100%*. And also that folding groovy stuff out of sticky notes is much more fun than Excel pivot tables. Your indisputable logic will defeat them and they will slink away, defeated, to the Human Resources department. You could also try converting them to the Path. The examples that Office Origami offers to all can be demonstrated through such events as the Business Card Frog Olympics or with a Shoot the Boss target range (introducing the latter to your actual boss is not recommended). An Executive Decision Maker folded from ordinary photocopy paper can determine the course of your co-worker's future careers and establish your own

reputation as a seer. Encourage them to become Office Origamists themselves, but make sure they buy their own copy of this sacred text. Remember, the wisdom contained within will not survive the photocopying process.

Your progress along the Path can be sped along by moving your desk closer to the stationery store, but consider also the good karma to be had from using paper that has come to the end of its life. Not only will you prevent vast swathes of rainforest from being razed, but in Office Origami the word "recycle" is synonymous with "reincarnate." Indeed, your efforts can breathe new life into paper once destined for crumpled perdition.

The following items are perfect for use in Office Origami:

- In-house magazines (badly) produced in a doomed attempt to inspire interest in the company and enthusiasm from staff.
- Meeting notes circulated by someone efficient in the forlorn hope that their organization and enthusiasm might be noticed.
- Any meeting notes in fact.
- Sticky notes left stuck to your desk and screen by people too "busy" to wait for you.
- The business cards of those you despise.
- Index cards, particularly if by removing a few at random you can ruin the system of a competitive co-worker, or anyone else who annoys you.
- Postcards from obsequious underlings (particularly if folded while they watch).
- Mission statements that would have you believe that the company's objectives are anything other than to make money and screw the competition.
- Any and all complaint letters.
- The mountain of junk mail, advertising catalogs, and hopeful resumés that you get every day.
- Contracts, legal letters, tax forms, and other vital documentation. Making Office Origami with this type of paper will immediately put the origamist on a much higher spiritual plane.

Be creative, nothing will show the boss how much you treasure his or her memos like a four-foot tower made exclusively from them.

The designs in this book include small practical projects that are paradoxical in nature. For example, in making the Boredom Box you are on the one hand creating origami that will keep your desk tidy and thus improve efficiency. However, in doing so you are, in fact, taking time that in the company's eyes would be more wisely spent calling clients. This presents a spiritual puzzle that you can ponder for many hours, or until 5.30pm at least.

Other designs are purely decorative, and projects such as Hippie Suncatcher should be employed to give your workspace the authentic feel of an Office Origami temple.

There are stress relieving projects for executives. Those around you will delight as over the days and weeks the Towers of Tokyo around and on your desk grow into a megalopolis; a megalopolis that might be devastated at any moment should you ever suffer a "Godzilla" moment during the working day. An assistant who triggers the destruction of an entire city by asking for an invoice to be signed will be wary of asking a second time.

The Way of Office Origami smiles upon its followers wasting time in a mildly amusing manner as much as it frowns upon sins of industriousness. With a range of potential Basketball Hoops, Paper Airplanes, Paper Firecrackers, and Hooplas just sitting in your in-tray waiting to be brought to life, you need never clock watch again! Indeed, with so many new and exciting ways of wasting time on offer you'd be tempted to get into the office early if this wasn't a deadly sin.

* Recent studies also indicate that the output and quality control of those producing amusing paper novelties after reading a copy of Office Origami that they own is as much as 134% higher than those who merely borrow it.

About Origami Diagrams

In order to become an Office Origami Master, you will need to understand the diagrams in this book, so pay attention, seeker of truth.

Origami diagrams are a sequence of "before" and "after" pictures that take you through the process of creating a paperfold one simple step at a time. Each picture in the diagrams is numbered to show the sequence in which they should be read. The process is so simple that the postroom boys could understand it, heck, even the vice-presidents.

The "before" pictures contain folding symbols that show you which part of the paper moves during the fold, where it ends up, and where the crease will form. The "after" pictures show you what the paper will look like once the fold has been made. To save on space many "after" pictures are also "before" pictures for the next

step in the sequence. This is possible through the power of Zenn diagrams, which are like Venn diagrams only they overlap in four dimensions of space and time.

The secret of reading origami diagrams is to always look at least one step ahead. If you know what the result of the fold should look like before you start to make it you are much more likely to get it right first time.

A basic folding instruction consists of a movement arrow and a foldline. The movement arrow tells you which part of the paper moves and which stays still, so that you know, for instance, whether to fold the right edge onto the left edge or vice versa. The fold line shows you exactly where the crease will form. Together, the two elements tell you everything else you need to know, such as whether the fold is made in front of or behind the paper. As you progess along the Path of Office Origami and become used to reading the diagrams this information will be sufficient in itself, but for the sake of clarity, and to make sure that no effort at all is required, the diagrams in this book are accompanied by written instructions, which make the meaning of the pictures crystal clear.

There are two special symbols that occur between pictures that you need to watch out for. The turnover symbol tells you that you need to turn the paper over—usually sideways—before making the next fold. The enlargement arrow tells you that the next picture has been drawn to a larger scale. It is particularly important that you watch out for turnover symbols. Not turning the paper over when you need to will make the rest of the design unnecessarily difficult—if not completely impossible—to fold.

The folding instructions are drawn as if the paper was laid on a hard flat surface like a desktop and you were looking down at it from above. You may find it easiest to follow the instructions with your paper laid out on a similar flat, hard surface such as your desk. It should first be cleared of all distracting clutter, as this will allow your thoughts to focus on the origami. This can be achieved through a process known to Office

Origamists as "delegation," though simply sweeping the contents of your desk into a wastebasket is an effective and quicker way of dealing with the problem.

Once you understand how a fold is to be made, you may find it more comfortable to turn the paper around to a different position or even to pick it up and make the fold in the air. The diagrams show you exactly what needs to be done but they don't necessarily show you the best way to do it. After practicing, everyone will find their own way of handling the paper, and what you should aim for is to be able to fold complex origami with one hand, while making coffee with the other and holding a conversation. Most co-workers will think you're a genius; some, a geek who needs to get out more. But the enlightened have always been persecuted.

One last piece of advice before we proceed. You do need to remember that once you have made a fold you need to carefully realign it to the diagrams before moving on.

A Guide to the Folding Symbols

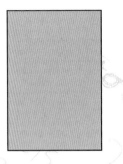

A The edges of the paper are shown as solid lines.

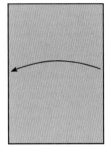

B The movement arrow shows the direction in which the fold is made.

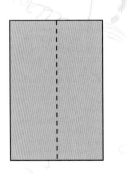

C The foldline shows where the new crease will form.

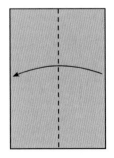

D A folding instruction consists of a movement arrow and a foldline. A combination of a solid movement arrow and a dotted foldline means the fold is made in front of the paper.

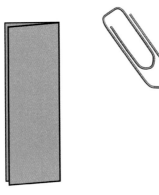

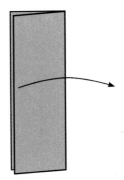

E This is the result of following the fold instruction in D. Edges that lie exactly on top of each other as the result of a fold are usually shown slightly offset on the after diagram, like this.

F A movement arrow without a foldline means unfold in the direction indicated.

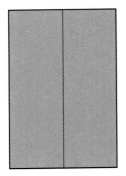

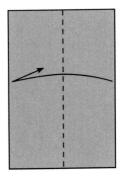

G Creases you have already made are shown as thin lines.

H Pictures D and F can be combined into a single instruction. This version of the movement arrow means fold, crease firmly, then unfold.

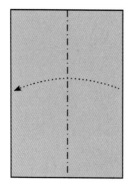

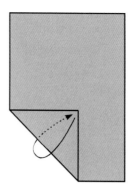

I A combination of a dotted movement arrow and a dashed and dotted foldline means the fold is made underneath the paper.

J A diagram of this kind tells you to swing the flap out of sight underneath the paper by reversing the direction of the existing crease.

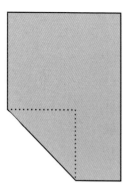

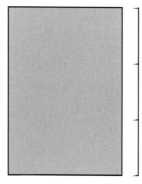

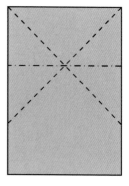

K This is the result of following instruction J. Dotted lines are sometimes used to show the edges of hidden flaps.

L This symbol shows how the adjacent edge can be seen as divided into a number of equal sections to help you locate a fold.

M A combination of the two types of foldline can be used to show you how the existing creases can be used to collapse the paper into a new shape.

N This symbol tells you to apply gentle pressure to the paper in the direction the arrowhead is pointing.

O This symbol tells you to move part of the paper in the direction of the arrow.

P The turnover symbol tells you to turn the paper over sideways.

Q The enlargement arrow tells you that the next diagram has been drawn to a larger scale.

R A circle is used to draw attention to some particular part of a picture that you need to look at carefully. Circles are also used as the boundaries of enlarged drawings where only part of the paper is shown.

S The eye symbol tells you that the next picture has been drawn as if you are looking at the design from the viewpoint shown.

How to Cut Squares From Rectangles

The One-Crease Method, using scissors

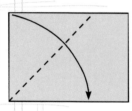

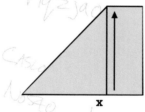

x

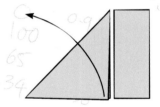

1 Fold the left hand edge onto the bottom edge. Hold the edges together and crease firmly.

2 Hold the sheets firmly together and in alignment—especially at point X—and cut carefully along the upright edge working from bottom to top.

3 Unfold the square.

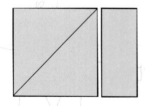

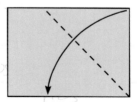

4 Squares made in this way have a single diagonal crease across them. You will find that this crease can often be reused when you are folding a design.

5 If you are left-handed you will probably find it easiest to make the initial fold in this direction, but the cut should still be made from bottom to top.

The No-Crease Method, using craft knife, metal rule, and cutting mat

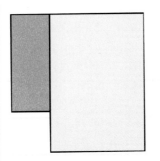

1 Line up the top and right hand edges of two sheets of paper exactly. Hold both sheets firmly in place.

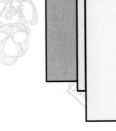

2 Lay a metal rule exactly along the left hand edge of the top sheet. Hold the rule firmly in place.

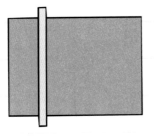

3 Remove the top sheet. Cut along the right hand edge of the metal rule taking great care that neither the rule nor the paper moves.

4 The result should be a perfect, uncreased square. If your knife is sharp enough you can cut several squares at a time in this way.

Basketball Hoop

This is quintessential Office Origami, the kind of project that not only kills a respectable number of office hours in perfecting and affords the folder hours of fun, but is so enjoyable that the whole company will want to try it.

Once you've made Basketball Hoop, shooting solitary hoops is a perfectly acceptable pastime—the imaginary crowds will go wild as you slam dunk that scrap of crumpled up paper while feigning interest to a client on the phone. However, the real beauty of Basketball Hoop is in watching its influence spread. Soon you will be having friendly competitions with the person at the next desk, trying to score through each other's hoops, and before you know it the whole office will have stopped work and there will be basketball tournaments going on everywhere you look. Even the most industrious will have a hard time resisting.

As you may be the only person with the instructions, the Hoop's popularity will mean a constant stream of requests, keeping you much too busy to respond to those emails that are piling up. However, a good ploy is to appear to be peeved about having to make so many: you're a busy professional! Co-workers pleading is always nice and you avoid the potentially damaging epithet of "ringleader."

Origin: This design probably started life as a playground fold in the USA. Nobody knows who first invented it, when, or where.

What to use: The Basketball Hoop can be folded from two photocopy-sized sheets of paper. One sheet forms the stand, the other the base. Balls can be scrunched up from any small scraps of paper, such as used message notes, you happen to have lying around.

Folding the Stand

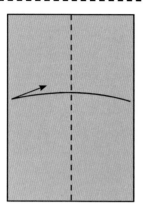

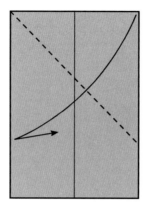

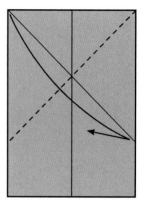

1 Fold in half from right to left, crease firmly, then unfold.

2 Fold the top edge onto the left hand edge, crease firmly, then unfold.

3 Fold the top edge onto the right hand edge, crease firmly, then unfold.

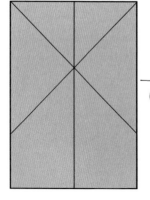

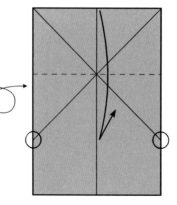

5 Create a horizontal crease that passes through the intersection of the two diagonal creases made in steps 2 and 3 by folding the top edge downward. The points where the diagonal creases intersect the right and left edges (marked with circles) can be used to locate this fold. Crease firmly, then unfold.

4 Turn over sideways.

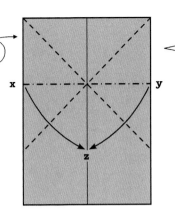

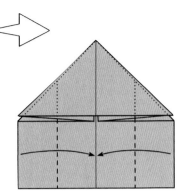

6 Turn over sideways.

7 Fold points x and y onto point z. Make both folds at the same time, using only the existing creases. If you have followed steps 1 through 5 correctly the paper will automatically collapse into the shape shown in picture 8.

8 Fold the left and right edges of the rear layers inward to lie along the vertical crease. Try to make sure you don't crease the front flaps as you do this.

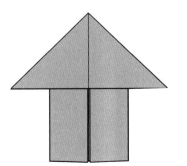

9 This is the result. It is time to add the base.

Adding
the base

10 Fold in half from right to left, crease firmly, then unfold.

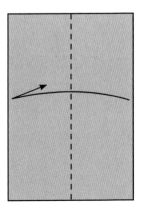

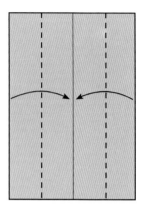

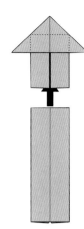

11 Fold both the right and left hand edges inward to lie along the vertical center crease.

12 Turn over sideways.

13 Push the base up inside the stand as far as it will go. The dotted line shows where the top of the base should end up. You may have to temporarily open out some of the folds of the stand to achieve this.

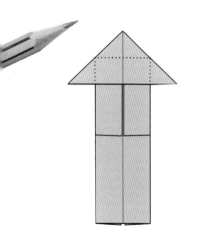

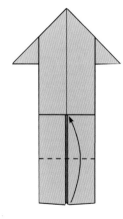

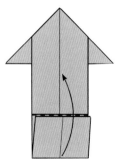

14 Turn over sideways.

15 Fold the bottom edge of the base upward to lie along the bottom edge of the stand.

16 Fold the new bottom edge of the base upwards using the bottom edge of the stand as a guide.

Forming the basket

- - - - - - - - - - - - -

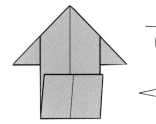

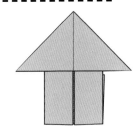

17 Turn over sideways.

18 To form the basket curl the front flaps upward and inward in the way shown in picture 19.

19 Insert the tip of one flap inside the other to form the basket. Slide the two flaps into each other until they are securely locked. There should be a small hole in the bottom of the basket.

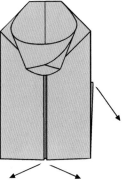

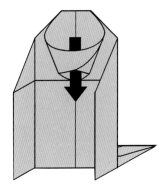

20 This is what the result should look like. Fold the tip of the top point backward to hold the sides of the basket apart.

21 Pull out the wings of the stand and lower the base behind. Allow the top layers of the base to spring upward slightly.

22 The Basketball Hoop is finished. Place on a desk top and bombard with small paper balls. The sprung stand will prevent the hoop falling over backward when you hit it.

Business Card Frog

There are so many business cards in circulation that the Business Card Frog should be a standard in every Office Origamist's repertoire. It is a great way of passing a few hours with colleagues, but perhaps its greatest contribution to Office Origami is in inflicting psychological damage on those unlucky enough to have a meeting with you.

It is common practice in today's business meetings to exchange cards as you exchange greetings. This gives a perfect opportunity for really effective non-verbal communication during the proceedings. If you become bored, or do not like what you are hearing, it takes no time to create a frog from the offender's business card. Now watch them squirm as you make it hop across the table and into the wastebasket. You can guarantee they won't be requesting a follow-up meeting, which means more time for Office Origami!

You can also organize sporting events with the frogs as competitors, and place bets. When arranging a day at the races in the office it is worth seeming altruistic and teaching co-workers how to make their own frogs (they will be more involved in the race and inclined to bet heavily). You, however, will have secretly placed your own frog on a training regimen to increase muscle mass. An, undetectable, extra piece of card will see your frog across the finish line in first place every time.

Origin: The Business Card Frog is a traditional Japanese design. (Though they probably didn't have business cards when it was first invented.)

What to use: You can make a Business Card Frog from stiff paper but your frog will jump much further if you make it from a small rectangle of lightweight card. Standard weight business cards are ideal.

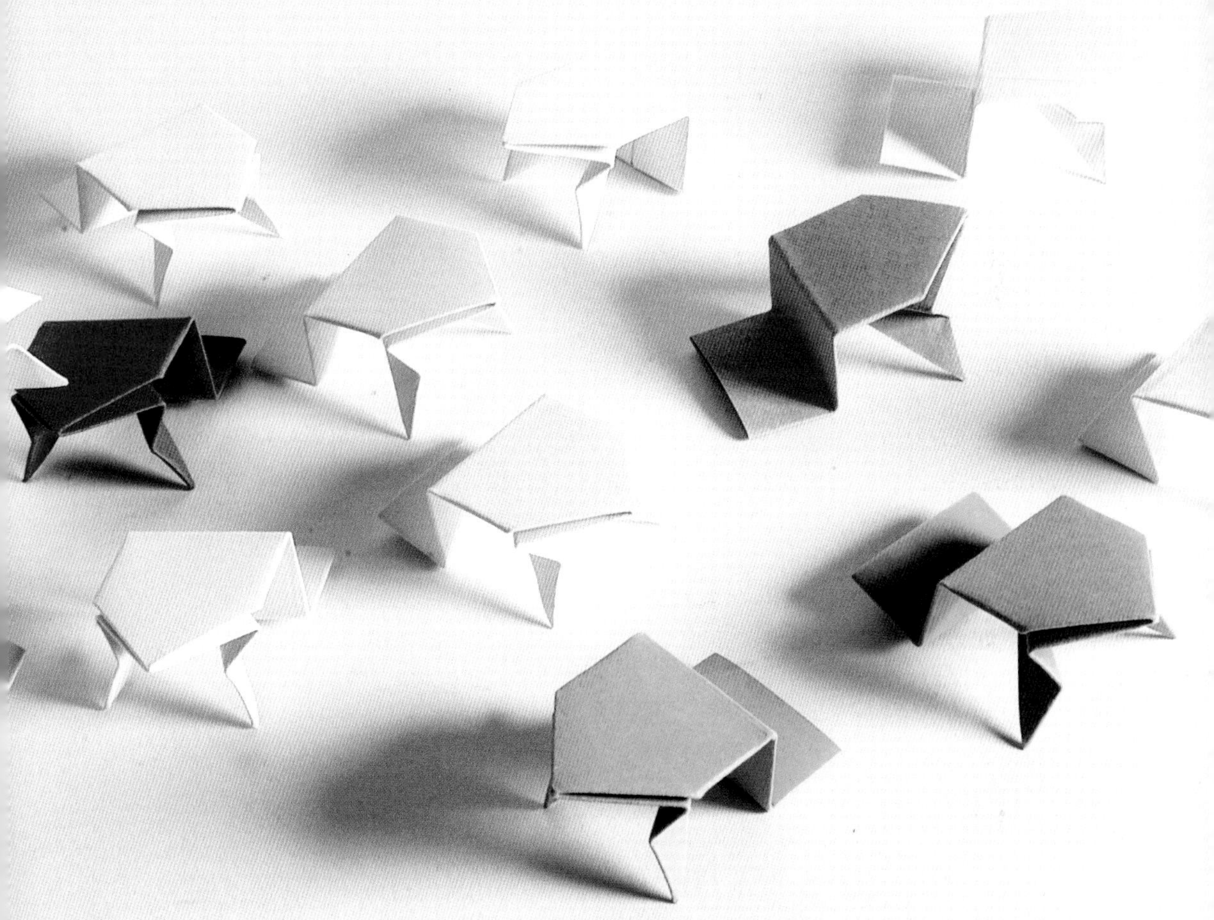

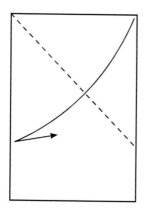

1 Fold the top edge onto the left hand edge, crease firmly, then unfold.

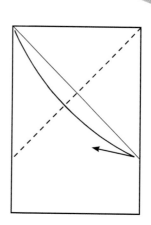

2 Fold the top edge onto the right hand edge, crease firmly, then unfold.

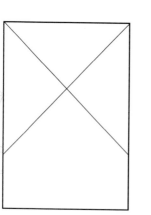

3 Turn over sideways.

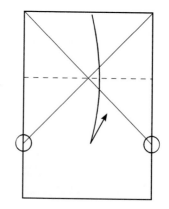

4 Create a horizontal crease that passes through the intersection of the two diagonal creases made in steps 1 and 2 by folding the top edge downward. The points where the diagonal creases intersect the right and left edges (marked with circles) can be used to locate this fold. Crease firmly, then unfold.

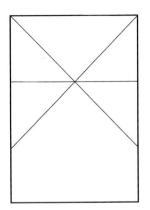

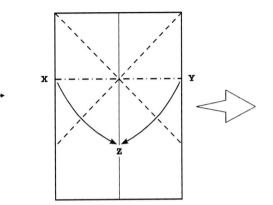

5 Turn over sideways.

6 Fold points x and y onto point z. Make both folds at the same time, using only the existing creases. If you have followed steps 1 through 5 correctly the card will automatically collapse into the shape shown in picture 7.

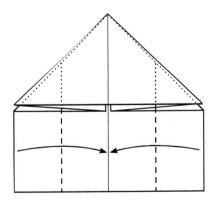

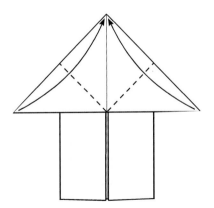

7 Fold the left and right edges of the rear layers inwards to lie along the vertical crease. Try to make sure you don't crease the front flaps as you do this.

8 Fold the left and right hand corners of the triangular flap up to the top point as shown.

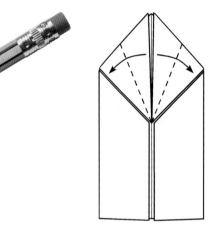

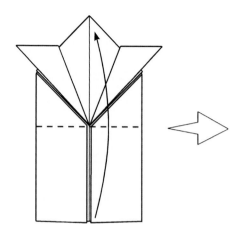

9 Fold the inside edges of both small triangular flaps outward again in the way shown here. Picture 10 shows what the result should look like.

10 Fold in half from bottom to top. This fold should only be creased softly. The next picture has been drawn to a larger scale.

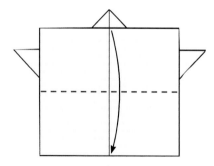

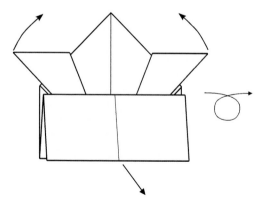

11 Fold the top layers in half from top to bottom. This fold should only be creased softly.

12 Allow the softly creased folds to spring open at right angles and open up the front legs to support the body. Turn the frog over and arrange like picture 13.

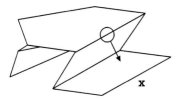

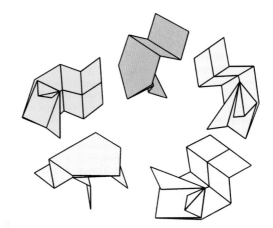

13 The back legs of the frog are the spring. To make your frog jump first compress the spring by pressing down on the frog's back with your index finger at the point marked with a circle, then release the tension by sliding your finger off backward. You may find it helps to achieve a better jump if you use your other hand to hold the base of the frog down at point x until the moment of release.

14 Business Card Frogs can land in one of five different positions. If racing frogs the rule is to set them upright with their front legs at the farthest point that they were in contact with the surface.

Putting your frog on steroids

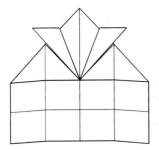

16 Open out the folds made in steps 7, 10, and 11 so that your frog looks like this.

17 Cut an extra piece of business card to about this size and slide it inside your frog. When you remake folds 7, 10, and 11 this extra piece will be concealed inside the folds. The spring will be more powerful so your frog will jump higher and further. If you are using your frog in competition you might be wise to keep this information to yourself.

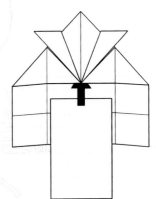

Shoot the Boss

This origami bust is a head and shoulders portrait of a largely faceless, short-necked, and empty-headed figure. Remind you of anyone?

Passed over for promotion? Small pay increase? Told to stop playing with paper and get on with some work? It is illegal to commit acts of violence on your superiors in the workplace, for more or less good reason; but this can lead to frustration and pent up feelings of rage that need a healthy outlet. Help is at hand with this handy desk boss. Drawing on the traditions of both Voodoo and the expressionist art of revolutionary Socialism it allows you to inflict your aggression on an effigy of the capitalist pig who bleeds you dry for a small amount of money.

If you pull the integral stand at the back out a little, The Boss will sit quite happily on a convenient desktop while you assault him (or her) with Weapons of Boss Destruction. Paper clips, rubber bands, paper balls or Origami Quoits can all be used as missiles. The important thing is that the target gets well and truly mangled. This won't matter. Like the real thing, The Boss is a readily replaceable item. All you need to do is fold another.

The design shown is the basic item, but can be personalized with a felt pen and a little imagination. We are told that in Haiti workers add a few tufts of the boss's hair, which magically transfers the wounds sustained by the effigy to the actual boss.

Just be careful that it remains hidden, as discovery could lead to awkwardness and even unemployment.

Origin: Designed by David Mitchell

What to use: You will need a single large square of paper. As square paper is unusual in offices this can be cut from any standard letter size sheet or rectangle using the techniques shown on pages 18 and 19.

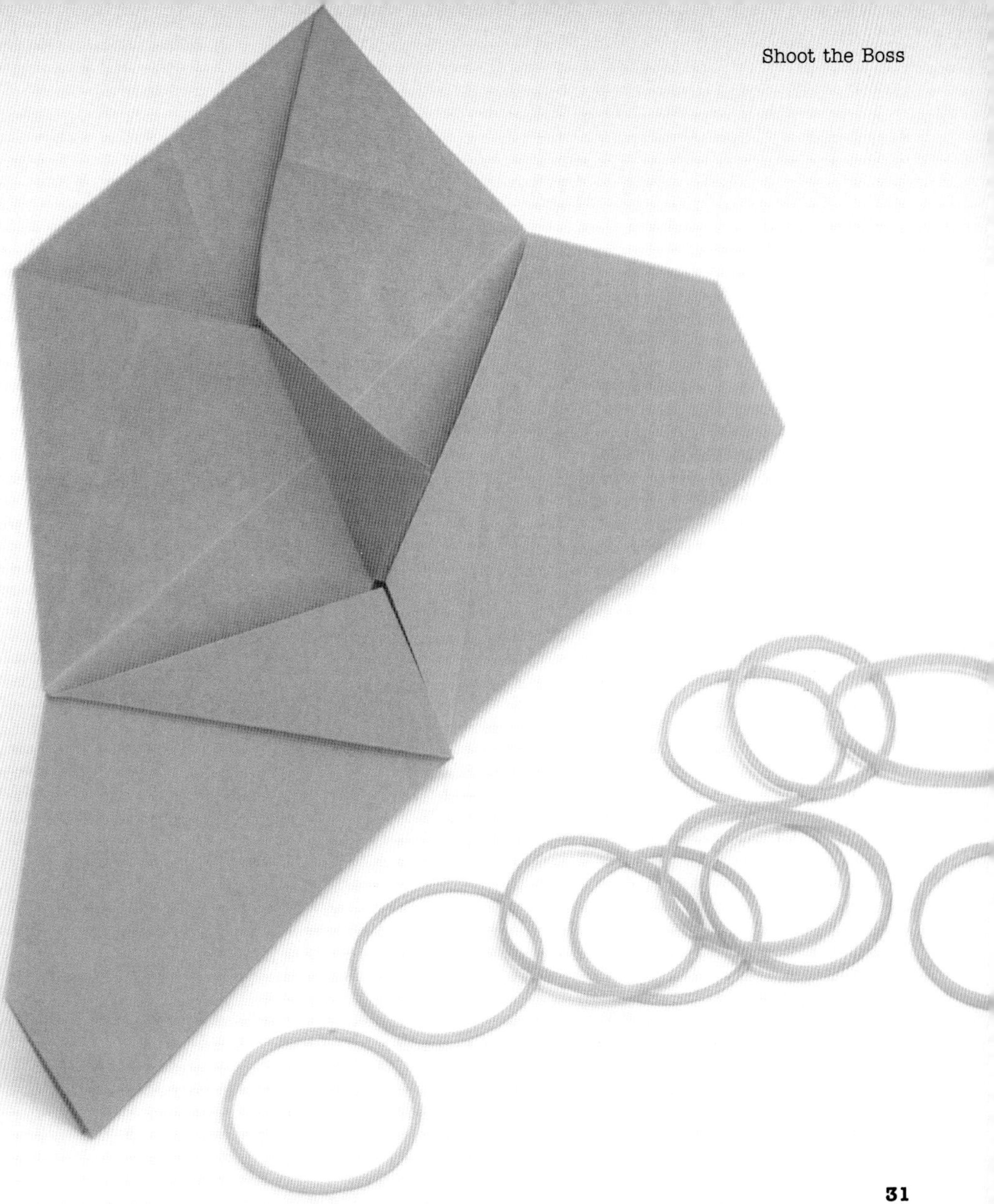

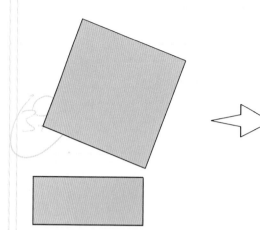

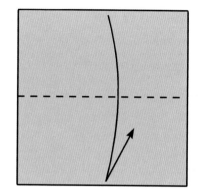

1 Begin with a large square cut from a sheet of rectangular paper. (See pages 16-17.)

2 Fold in half from top to bottom, crease firmly, then unfold.

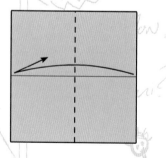

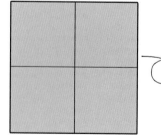

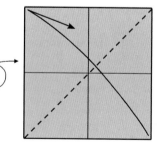

3 Fold in half from right to left, crease firmly, then unfold.

4 Turn over sideways.

5 Fold in half diagonally, crease firmly, then unfold.

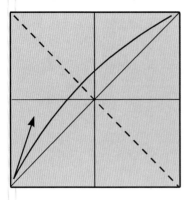

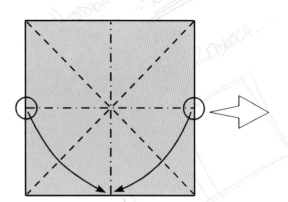

6 Fold in half diagonally in the other direction, crease firmly, then unfold.

7 Fold both points marked with circles onto the center of the bottom edge. Make both folds at the same time, using only the existing creases. If you have followed steps 2 through 6 correctly the paper will collapse into the shape shown in picture 8.

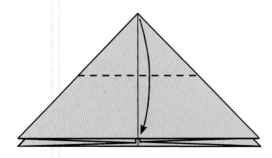

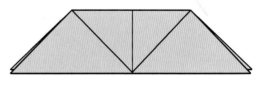

8 Fold in half from top to bottom.

9 Turn over sideways.

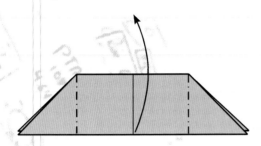

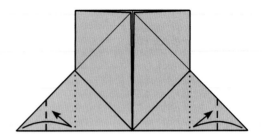

10 Open the front layers upward then flatten them so that your paper looks like picture 11.

11 Fold both outside corners inwards as shown, crease firmly, then unfold.

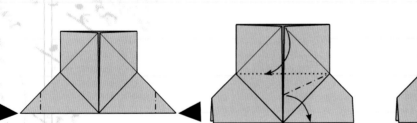

12 Turn the points inside out in between the other layers.

13 Lift up front layer on the right hand side and squash it flat in the position shown in picture 14. You will need to make two new creases as you flatten the paper into position.

14 This is the result. Tuck the tip of the front right hand layer underneath the front left hand layer.

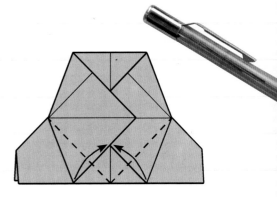

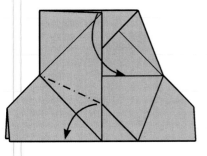

15 Repeat step 13 on the front left hand layer of the paper.

16 Form the collars of the Boss's shirt by making these two small folds.

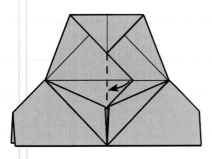

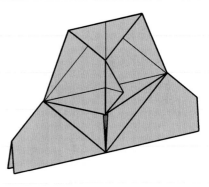

17 Fold the tip of the point of the front layer towards you at right angles to form a rudimentary nose.

18 If you pull out the stand (at the back) slightly The Boss will sit happily on any flat surface while you bombard him or her.

Boredom Box

What better way to demonstrate your efficiency while actually doing very little than by painstakingly tidying your desk. Completed to a standard that conforms to your company's expectations of excellence, desk tidying can take up to a week. The Boredom Box can help really string out that time. So named because it is an easy design for those moments of true ennui when you can't even face reading a set of instructions, you only have to do it once to get the hang of it. It will also make your paper clips and elastic bands look alluring.

Origin: The Boredom Box is a traditional American design sometimes known as the Magazine Cover Box. The strengtheners are a design revamp by David Mitchell.

What to use: The instructions show you how to make the Box from a letter size sheet of photocopy paper, but virtually any other rectangle of any other kind of paper or light card will do equally well. If you want to get noticed, try using your latest employee evaluation.

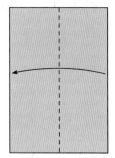

1 Fold in half from right to left. Crease firmly.

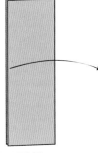

2 Unfold.

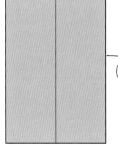

3 Turn over sideways.

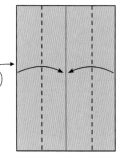

4 Fold the right and left hand edges inward to lie along the vertical center crease.

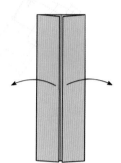

5 Unfold.

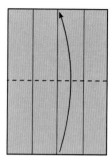

6 Fold in half from bottom to top. Crease firmly.

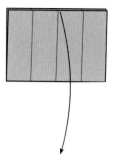

7 Unfold.

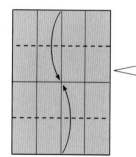

8 Fold the top and bottom edges inward to lie on the horizontal center crease.

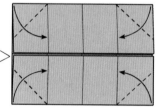

9 Fold all four corners inward using the vertical creases made in step 4 as a guide.

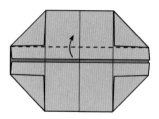

10 There are two loose flaps in the center of the design. Fold the upper flap upward as far as it will go to lock the triangular flaps created in step 9 in place.

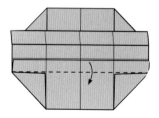

11 This is the result. Repeat step 10 on the lower edge.

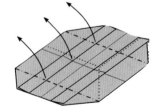

12 Lift one of the shorter sides into place as shown. The rest of the box will now begin to take shape. Rework the corner creases to establish the shaps by the dotted lines.

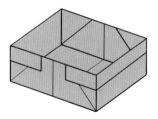

13 The Box is finished.

Strengthening the sides

If you have made your Boredom Box from light card it will be strong enough as it is. If you have made it from paper you will find that the longer sides of the box are quite weak and you may wish to reinforce it by adding a strengthening piece folded from a second sheet of paper like this.

Begin by following steps 1 through 8 of the Box then continue with steps 14 through 17 here.

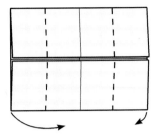

14 Swing the right and left hand flaps forward at right angles using the existing creases.

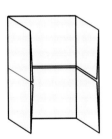

15 The strengthening piece is finished.

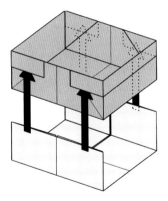

16 Tuck the edges of the strengthening piece into the pockets on the longer sides of the box as shown.

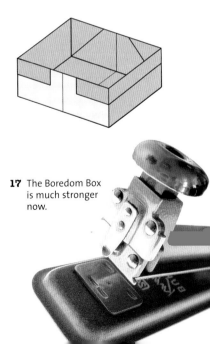

17 The Boredom Box is much stronger now.

Water Cooler Cup

This is Office Origami at its smoothest. Water cooler cup dispenser unfilled again; who does everyone turn to for their liquid receptacle needs? Not enough glasses to go round at the office party; who *is* that elegantly sipping champagne from Thursday's budget meeting notes. The answer to these questions is YOU. While all around you there is panic, like a certain spy trying out the latest gadget you will be putting together a stylish little paper cup, just the right size for a martini. With practice you might even be able to do it with one hand, a feat that will have the opposite sex in a whirl.

It is rumored in paperfolding circles that this design was once classed as restricted information by the US Government, presumably as it was considered dangerously sexy. Another version of the story has it that the design once featured in a US Army survival manual. These are tales that are worth recounting at the water cooler while

you fold. Your audiences will be entranced by your repartée, and will also believe that you have access to classified information, or at least have studied the Army survival manual. Your already high sex appeal will skyrocket. You should just smile knowingly.

A couple of caveats. First, the cup can only be used once. Second, and most important, don't use it for hot drinks. These may scald you when you either drop the cup to lick your burning fingers or the hot liquid drops out of the bottom onto your lap. Either scenario results in the erosion of the desired air of composure.

Origin: The One Time Cup is a traditional Japanese design.

What to use: A sheet of letter size photocopy paper is ideal. It is actually probably best not to use scrap paper or meeting notes since office printer inks are often water-soluble.

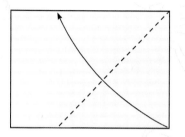

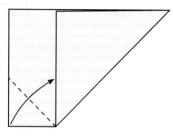

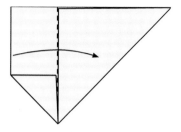

1 Fold the right hand edge onto the top edge as shown. Crease firmly.

2 Fold the lower left hand corner inward using the vertical edge of the triangular flap as a guide.

3 Fold the left hand edge inward using the vertical edge of the large triangular flap as a guide.

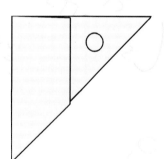

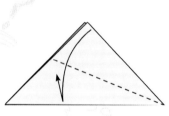

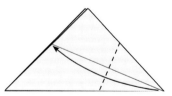

4 Rearrange the layers to bring the large triangular flap (marked with a circle) to the top. Align to picture 5.

5 Fold the right hand sloping edge of the top layer down to lie along the bottom edge, crease firmly, then unfold.

6 Fold the right hand corner onto the point where the crease made in step 5 intersects the sloping left hand edge.

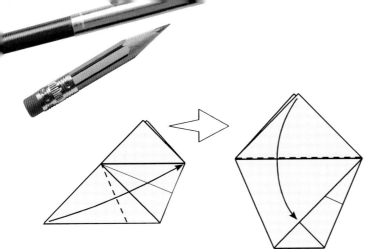

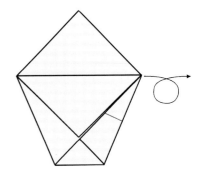

7 Fold the left hand corner inward in a similar way. The next picture is on a larger scale.

8 Fold the front flap down in front using the top edges of the triangular flaps as a guide.

9 The triangular flaps are now locked in place. Turn over sideways.

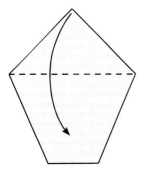

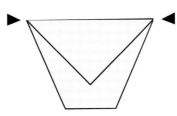

10 Fold the top corner down in a similar way.

11 The cup is finished. Press the corners toward each other to open the top.

12 Fill with water, cola, juice, or champagne. Use with coffee or other hot drinks is not recommended; disastrous in fact.

Frog Eat Frog

Some Office Origami designs have practical applications, relieving stress or inflicting cruelty on those around you. This however, is a simple novelty suitable for entertaining those of limited mental faculties such as very small children or senior management. Imagine their trusting little faces all aglow with delight and amazement as they see the big frog has eaten a little frog!

It can also be used as an impromptu birthday card for anyone you don't like. This will send out the following messages:

1. You forgot.
2. When you were reminded you couldn't be bothered to make a trip to the store for a card or a gift.
3. You're also too cheap to buy one.

The beauty is that the recipient will know all this and have to thank you anyway. There is a marvelous tradition in our society—and one that the Office Origamist can take complete advantage of—that if a gift is handmade it shows you care more than someone who went shopping, picked out a suitable gift, and paid hard-earned money for it. Though they'll secretly be cursing you the recipient will risk looking rude and ungrateful if they don't thank you effusively when you present your "special card." In this way Office Origami will gently train you to be a penny-pinching, cheapskate swine. Your place on the board is virtually assured.

Frog Eat Frog is best given to those you have the power to fire if they do not make suitable noises of gratitude and amazement at your talent.

Origin: Developed by Oliver Zachary.

What to use: Frog Eat Frog is best folded (and cut) from a single sheet of green or yellow photocopy size paper or US letter size paper.

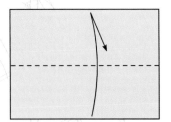

1 Fold in half from bottom to top, crease firmly, then unfold.

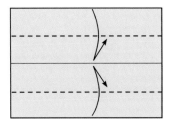

2 Fold the top and bottom edges inward to lie along the horizontal center crease, crease firmly, then unfold.

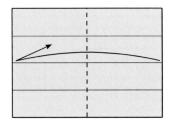

3 Fold in half from right to left, crease firmly, then unfold.

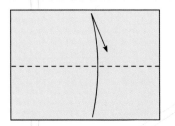

4 Fold the right and left edges inward to lie along the vertical center crease, crease firmly, then unfold.

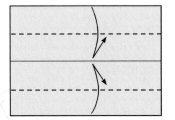

5 Fold in half from right to left using the crease made in step 3.

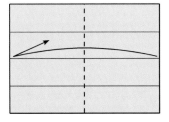

6 Fold the top and bottom right hand corners inward using the horizontal creases as a guide. Crease firmly.

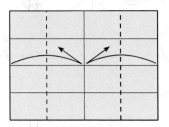

7 Open out the folds made in step 6.

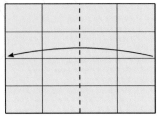

8 Push both corners inside out between the other layers using the creases made in step 6.

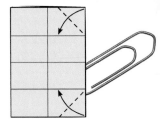

9 This is the result. Crease the edges firmly. Follow the instructions in the enlargements to create the first frog.

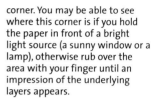

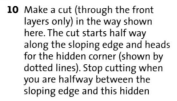

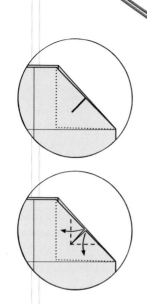

10 Make a cut (through the front layers only) in the way shown here. The cut starts half way along the sloping edge and heads for the hidden corner (shown by dotted lines). Stop cutting when you are halfway between the sloping edge and this hidden corner. You may be able to see where this corner is if you hold the paper in front of a bright light source (a sunny window or a lamp), otherwise rub over the area with your finger until an impression of the underlying layers appears.

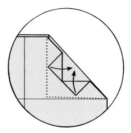

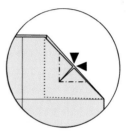

11 Make the two small folds shown here. The creases should be parallel to the edges of the hidden flaps.

12 Open out the folds you made in step 11.

13 Push both flaps inside out between the other layers using the creases made in step 11. Crease firmly.

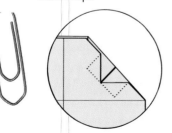

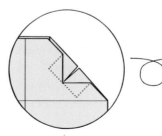

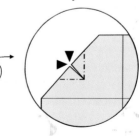

14 Make a cut through the back layers to match the cut you made in the front layers in step 10. This cut is easier to make since you can use the front layers as a guide.

15 Turn over sideways.

16 Repeat steps 11 through 13 on this pair of flaps. Don't forget to crease firmly again.

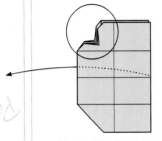

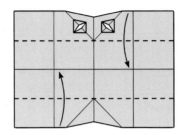

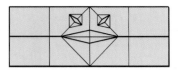

19 The first frog is finished.

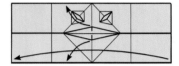

17 Swing the back layers of the design into view without turning the paper over. Be careful not to flatten any of the folds.

18 Fold the top and bottom edges inward using the existing creases.

20 Begin making the second frog by folding the paper in half from right to left. Make sure the folds of the frog's mouth and eyes swing out into their fully open position again as you do this.

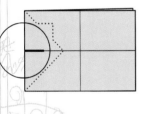

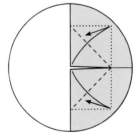

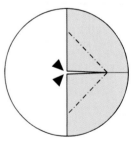

21 The dotted line shows the hidden edges of the inside layers of paper. Before you make this cut check that all the edges do in fact lie in the position shown. (See step 10 for how to find the edges of the hidden layers). This cut goes roughly halfway to the apex of the hidden layers. Once you have made the cut follow the instructions in the enlargements to create the second frog.

22 Fold the corners released by the cut inward so that they end up in the positions marked by the dotted lines, crease firmly, then unfold.

23 Push both flaps inside out between the layers using the creases made in step 22. Crease firmly.

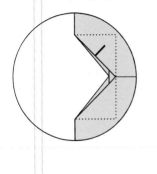

24 This is the result. Make another tiny cut (through the front layers only) in the way shown here. This move is a repeat of step 10. Continue to form the second frog by repeating steps 11 through 16 as well.

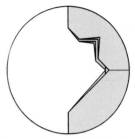

25 The result should look like this. Crease all the edges firmly.

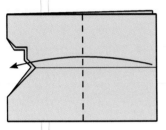

26 Using the existing crease, fold the right hand edge of the front layers across to the left.

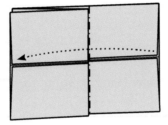

27 Using the existing crease, fold the remaining right hand edge across to the left behind the other layers of the paper.

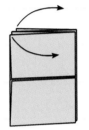

28 Crease all the edges, including the edges of the internal layers, firmly once more, then swing the front and back flaps out at right angles.

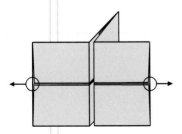

29 Grasp a flap in either hand and pull gently apart.

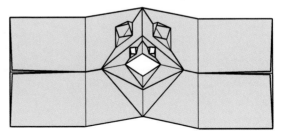

30 Be careful! It's a Frog Eat Frog world out there.

Paper Firecracker

The Paper Firecracker is a wonderful way of attracting attention to yourself. It will also irritate the hell out of anyone within earshot. We cannot think of two better reasons for this to become a staple for any Office Origamist.

Paper Firecracker's uses are manifold. Imagine your secretary's or assistant's response when they are summoned to your office by its resonant explosion rather than a boring old phone call! If you're lucky enough to have an underling that you can abuse in this way it is also worth noting that different papers make slightly different qualities of bang. Why not use a range of firecrackers to signal different requests, for example the brash sound of the magazine firecracker means "coffee," the crisp tabloid means "book lunch," and the quieter, more peaceful pop of last week's presentation means "hold my calls." You'll enjoy teaching them to respond to the different sounds almost as much as

you'll enjoy gently remonstrating with them when they get it wrong.

If you don't have a secretary then don't despair. Paper Firecracker is great for making unwitting victims jump out of their skins. By the time they've turned round you'll simply be looking at a finance report. For the more outgoing, nothing brings all eyes around a meeting table back to you more quickly or effectively. Just make sure you can follow it up with something worth saying.

On wet afternoons you may enjoy having "gunfights" with your co-workers. The dead get coffee.

Origin: The paper Banger is a traditional Japanese design. Those Japanese, eh?

What to use: Paper Bangers can be folded from sheets of photocopy size or US letter size paper. Scrap paper is ideal. Some papers make a louder noise than others. Experiment widely and loudly.

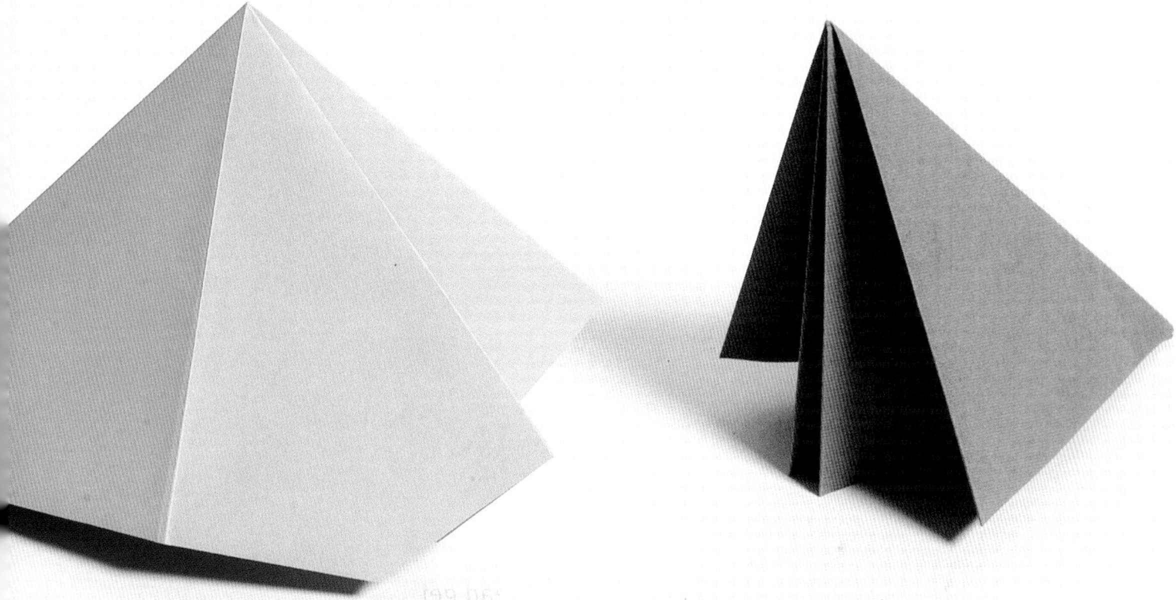

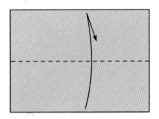

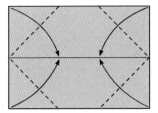

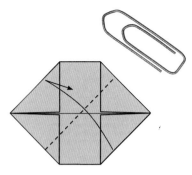

1 Fold in half from bottom to top, crease firmly, then unfold.

2 Fold all four corners inward using the horizontal center crease as a guide.

3 Fold in half diagonally as shown, crease firmly, then unfold.

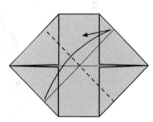

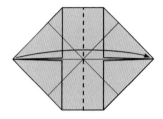

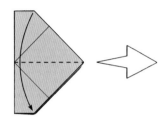

4 Fold in half diagonally in the alternative direction, crease firmly, then unfold.

5 Fold in half from left to right.

6 Fold in half from top to bottom using the crease made in step 1.

Loading the Paper Firecracker

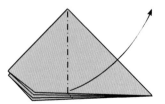

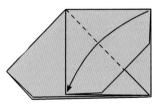

7 The Paper Firecracker is folded and ready for loading.

8 Open up the front pocket by folding the center of the bottom edge (of the front layer only) upward to the right. The left hand point of the pocket will flatten to look like picture 9.

9 Fold the top right hand corner back to its starting position to trap the original left hand point inside the layers.

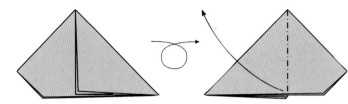

10 The first barrel is loaded. Turn over sideways.

11 Open up the new front pocket by folding the center of the bottom edge (of the front layers only) upward to the left. The right hand point will flatten to look like picture 12.

12 Fold the top left hand corner back to its starting position to trap the original right hand point between the layers.

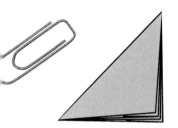

13 Both barrels are loaded. The Paper Firecracker is finished.

Firing and reloading the Paper Firecracker

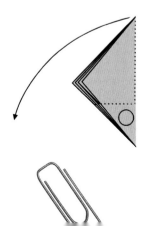

14 Grip the Paper Firecracker firmly between your thumb and first finger at the position marked with the circle so that the internal flaps are free to move. Fire the Paper Firecracker by flicking your arm and wrist sharply downward in the direction of the arrow. As you do this air pressure will cause the internal flaps to flip out, making a surprisingly loud noise as they do so.

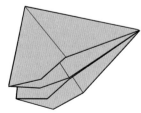

15 You can reload the Paper Firecracker by repeating steps 8 through 12.

Snap Dragon

Interdesk missiles are always fun and also help your co-workers to forget about work and focus on angles of aerial attack. This flying dragon, best made from index cards, is guaranteed to evoke hilarity. Especially when you steal those cards from someone's prized system and spend the day sending them flying back one by precious one. The strength of the spring is dependent on climatic conditions—it won't perform well in hot, humid conditions, but in cool dry places Snap Dragon has been known to fly some 13–16 feet or even more.

Origin: The Snap Dragon presented here is a variation of an original design by the American paperfolder Dorothy Engleman.

What to use: Snap Dragon was designed to be made from a standard 3" x 5" index card, but, if you have very nimble fingers you could try folding it from a thin business card instead.

1 Fold in half from right to left, crease firmly, then unfold.

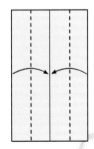

2 Fold the right and left hand edges inward to lie along the crease made in step 1.

3 Create Snap Dragon's head by following the instructions in the enlargements.

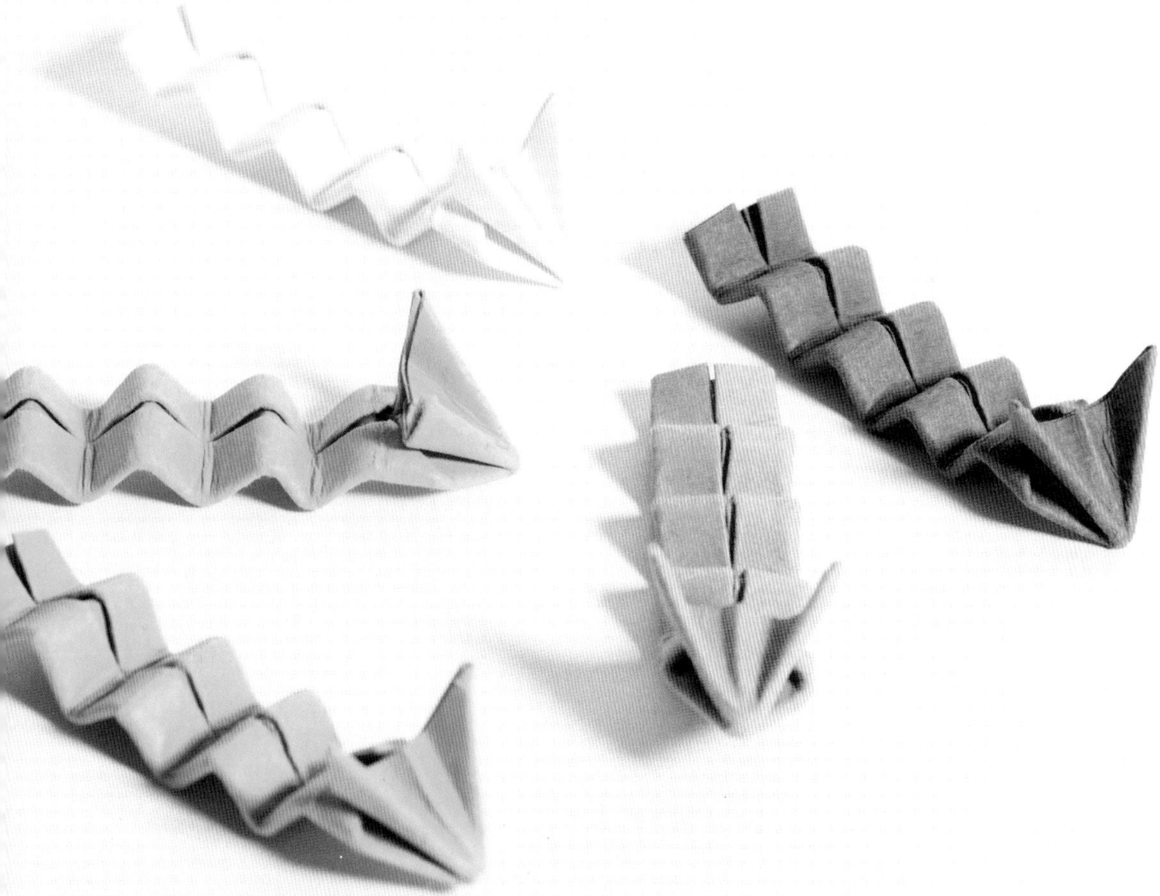

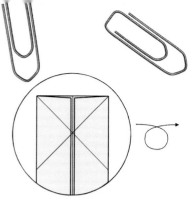

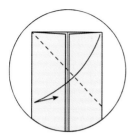

4 Fold the top edge diagonally downward to lie along the left hand edge, crease firmly, then unfold.

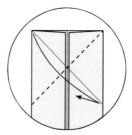

5 Fold the top edge diagonally downward to lie along the right hand edge, crease firmly, then unfold.

6 Turn over sideways.

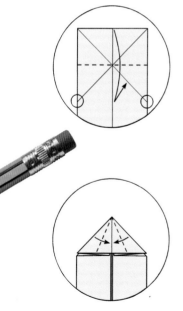

7 Create a horizontal crease that passes through the intersection of the diagonal creases made in steps 5 and 6 by folding the top edge downward. The points where the diagonal creases intersect the right and left edges (marked with circles) can be used to locate this fold. Crease firmly, then unfold. Turn over sideways again.

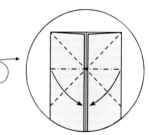

8 Collapse the top into the form shown in picture 9 using the existing creases.

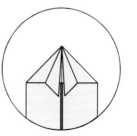

9 Form Snap Dragon's horns by making these two tiny folds.

10 This is the result.

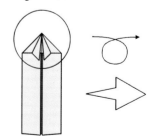

11 Turn over sideways. The next picture has been drawn on a larger scale.

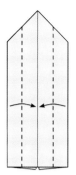  

12 Fold the right and left edges inward to lie along the vertical center crease.

13 Fold the top point downward so that the head comes into view.

14 Turn over sideways.

15 Fold the remainder of the strip into a zig-zag spring using the top of the strip and the point where the edge of the head changes direction as guides. Make the folds softly so that the spring will have some zip left in it. Picture 16 shows what the result should look like.

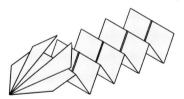

16 Snap Dragon is finished.

17 To make Snap Dragon fly first tuck the tip of your thumb in between the horns on the top of the head then compress the concertina folds with your middle finger so that Snap Dragon forms into a spring. Squeeze the folds tightly, then snap your thumb off the head onto your finger to suddenly release the tension in the spring. Snap Dragon will fly away. With practice you will be able to make Snap Dragon fly quite a surprising distance. Controlling the direction of the flight is quite another thing.

The Naughty Elephant

Anyone who has worked in an office environment will be familiar with that sense of conflict during times of great stress between what you really think and professional restraint. Those moments when all you want to do is shout "WHAT THE *!$*& ARE YOU TALKING ABOUT YOU *!$*&ING IDIOT," but you know that to do so would incur the displeasure of the HR department. You will be pleased to know that Office Origami has the perfect solution and is pleased to offer the Naughty Elephant for your relief.

It works like so. Upside down it looks like an elephant head represented in origami. It is an innocent little device, not taking too much time to fold and it even hangs on your computer monitor. So far so good. This elephant head should become your personal mascot. Your boss and co-workers should get used to seeing it around your desk. You may also like to make more elephant heads absent-mindedly in meetings.

But what's this! Someone disagrees with you, or is dismissive of your efforts, or makes undue demands on you. Where previously your rage had no outlet, now when someone has upset you, you will find that you've accidently flipped your elephant head over. And it looks like you're giving them the finger! Oh me oh my.

Although great when you need to vent a little spleen behind someone's back, the Naughty Elephant works best when your antagonist sees it. They'll know, and you'll know, but to HR you'll have simply knocked your elephant head over. "It looked like a finger? Boy, I hadn't even noticed. Some people are really sensitive, huh?"

Origin: Designed by Oliver Zachary.

What to use: You will need a single small square cut from quite stiff paper.

1 Begin with a small square cut from a sheet of photocopy size or US letter size paper.

2 Fold in half from right to left, crease firmly, then unfold.

3 Fold in half from top to bottom making only the tiniest of creases, then unfold. If you prefer you can omit this step and make fold 4 as a judgement fold by eye alone.

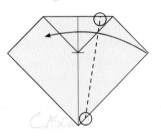

4 Fold the top corner downward using the intersection of the creases made in steps 2 and 3 to locate the fold.

5 Fold the right hand corner across to the left. There are no location points for this fold, which must be made by eye alone. Picture 6 shows what the result should look like.

6 Turn over sideways.

7 Fold the right hand corner across to the left by reversing the direction of the existing crease.

8 Fold the left hand corner across to the right so that the edges of the front and back flaps line up exactly. Crease firmly.

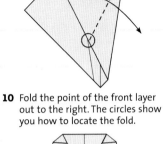

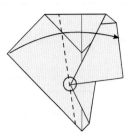

9 Undo folds 7 and 8 and return the paper to the alignment shown in picture 6.

10 Fold the point of the front layer out to the right. The circles show you how to locate the fold.

11 Fold the left hand point back across to the right using the existing crease.

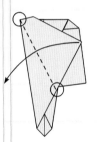

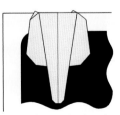

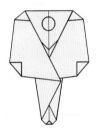

12 Fold the point of the front layer out to the left. This is a repeat of step 10. Try to maintain the symmetry of the design as you make this fold.

13 Make these three small folds to round off the ears and the tip of the trunk.

14 Gently release the flap marked with a circle from the other layers and lift it up toward you at right angles.

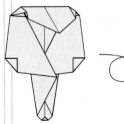

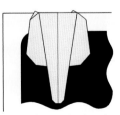

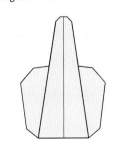

15 Your elephant mascot is finished. Turn over sideways.

16 Use the flap to hang the head from a suitable shelf or VDU.

17 Whoops-a-daisy.

Origami Quoits

Origami Quoits are an essential component of your desktop sporting environment. These square-shaped rings are folded from long strips of paper and will fly a surprisingly distance if launched sideways with a flick of the wrist. Origami Quoits can be used as hoops to juggle with, for a simple game of catch, for playing Rhino Hoopla, or as missiles for a game of Shoot The Boss. The bigger you make your Origami Quoits the greater the range of targets you can attempt.

Origin: Designed by David Mitchell.

What to use: Long strips cut from rectangles of any kind of paper. Quoits made from strips cut from photocopy size or US letter size paper will work perfectly well but quoits made from longer strips will work much better.

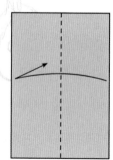

1 Fold in half from right to left, crease firmly, then unfold.

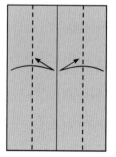

2 Fold both the right and left hand edges inward to lie along the vertical center crease, crease firmly, then unfold.

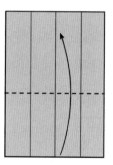

3 Fold the bottom edge upward like this. Picture 4 shows what the result should look like.

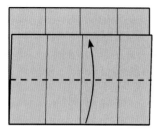 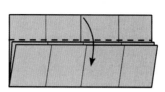 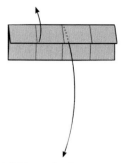

4 Fold the new bottom edge upward to lie along the original bottom edge.

5 Fold the top edge downward as far as it will go. Crease firmly.

6 Unfold completely.

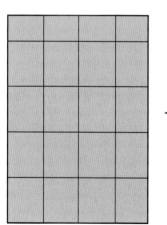 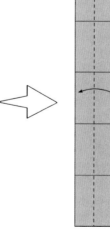

7 Cut your paper into four thin strips along the vertical creases. Each strip will become a quoit.

8 Fold in half from right to left.

9 Fold in half from right to left once more.

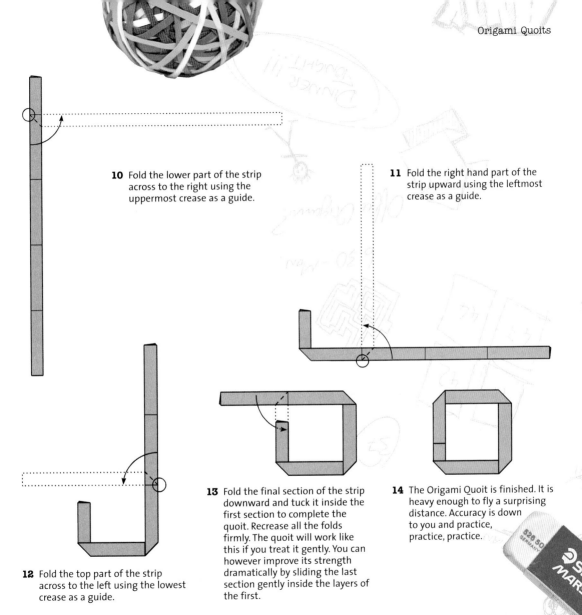

10 Fold the lower part of the strip across to the right using the uppermost crease as a guide.

11 Fold the right hand part of the strip upward using the leftmost crease as a guide.

13 Fold the final section of the strip downward and tuck it inside the first section to complete the quoit. Recrease all the folds firmly. The quoit will work like this if you treat it gently. You can however improve its strength dramatically by sliding the last section gently inside the layers of the first.

14 The Origami Quoit is finished. It is heavy enough to fly a surprising distance. Accuracy is down to you and practice, practice, practice.

12 Fold the top part of the strip across to the left using the lowest crease as a guide.

Rhino Hoopla

Roll Up, Roll Up. Ladies and gentlemen—put down that calculator ma'am—we present a new pant-wetting, side-splitting game, suitable for any office that has a pad of sticky notes.

The universal truth of offices is that they are dull places. The people working in them, no matter how many motivational seminars they've been on, would always rather be doing something else. This is an environment ripe for distraction. And there's none tougher to resist than the fairground fun of Rhino Hoopla.

Of course, you can play it on your own by sticking the rhinos to a convenient wall and flicking quoits at them while some inconsiderate idiot drones on at you down the phone. It passes the time in a not unpleasant way. But the real joy of Rhino Hoopla is in knowing you are responsible for the surreal sight of a roomful of mature, responsible people standing around in business suits with sticky note rhinos stuck to their heads and throwing

paper quoits at each other. If you can achieve this then enlightenment is yours.

It is not easy though, there will always be one or two diehards who will sniff at enjoying themselves. However, it is possible to make even these joyless fools join in by pitching Rhino Hoopla as a "team building" exercise. Another universal truth of offices is that any pastime, no matter how stupid, will be readily accepted if it's presented as "team building." People will walk barefoot on hot coals rather than be thought of as anything other than a fully paid-up team player.

Origin: Concept and design by David Mitchell.

What to use: 3 x 5" message notes are ideal. If larger targets are preferred you can fold them from ordinary paper and attach them to a suitable surface with sticky tape or drawing pins.

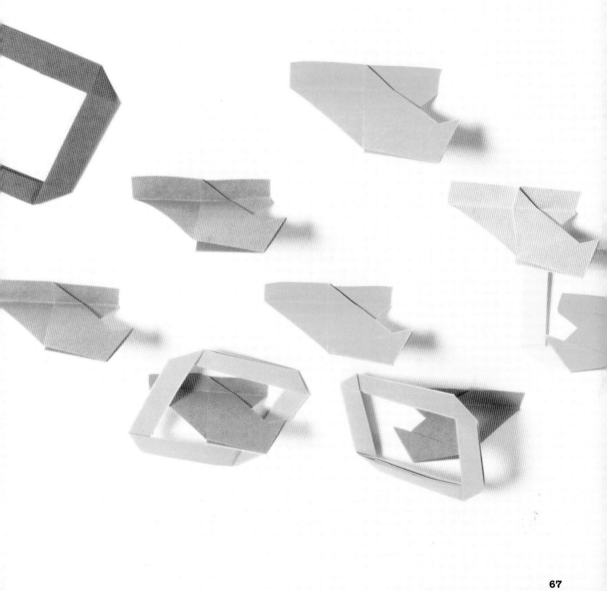

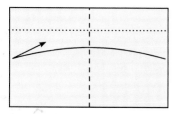

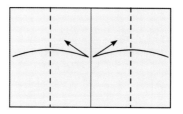

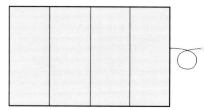

1 If you are using 3 x 5" message notes make sure the sticky strip is at the top behind the paper. Fold in half from right to left, crease firmly, then unfold.

2 Fold both right and left edges inward to lie along the vertical center crease, crease firmly, then unfold.

3 Turn over sideways.

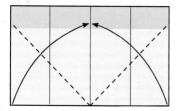

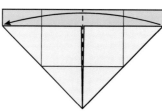

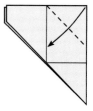

4 Fold both bottom corners inward using the vertical center crease as a guide.

5 Fold in half from right to left using the existing crease.

6 Fold the top right hand corner inward using the vertical crease as a guide.

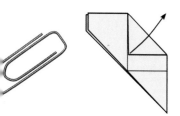

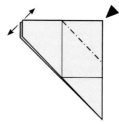

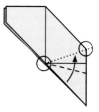

7 Crease firmly then unfold.

8 Open the top of the paper and turn the top right hand corner inside out between the layers using the creases made in step 6.

9 Fold the bottom right hand corner upward as shown. Picture 10 shows what the result should look like.

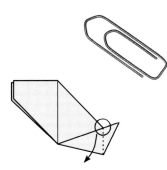

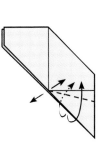

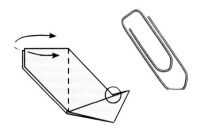

10 Crease firmly then unfold.

11 Open out the left hand side of the paper and turn the point inside out outside the other layers using the creases made in step 9.

12 Open out the two left hand flaps at right angles in front and behind.

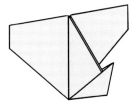

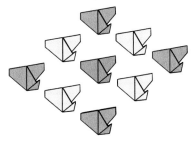

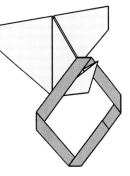

13 The Rhino target is finished. If you have made it from a message note you will be able to stick it to a convenient wall, window or forehead using the sticky strip. If you have made it from ordinary paper you will need to attach it in some other way. Drawing pins are not recommended for foreheads.

14 Rhino are sociable animals. The dominant (higher scoring) animals are often found in the center of the group.

15 A successful shot. Harder than it looks. Especially when the Rhino is charging.

Executive Decision Maker

Ever wonder how top business executives come across so cool and calm, able to make those smart, snappy decisions, and with such panache? Well now their secret is revealed. The construction of the Executive Decision Maker is taught at top business schools throughout the world, from Harvard to the London School of Economics. It allows the user to choose between eight preselected decisions in an entirely stress free way, leaving them time to worry about important things, like what brand of hair gel to use and white collar crime.

Now you too can use this great method to take decisions that are completely untainted by the slightest bias (whether caused by accurate information, economic necessity, empathy with your fellow humans, or any other kind of contact with external reality).

To reduce your stress levels still further we have provided a comprehensive set of pre-planned decisions for you to use, so that whether you are a worker, manager, or already have your feet firmly on the top rung of the executive ladder you can sit back, disengage your brain, and put your fingers firmly in charge of your destiny (and that of your company).

Origin: The Executive Decision Maker is a traditional paperfold known as the Saltcellar. You may remember using it as a Fortune Teller or Cootie Catcher in the playground at school.

What to use: You will need a single large square of paper cut from an photocopy size or US letter size sheet and a pen to add the numbers with.

Pre-selected decisions

Workers

1 Complain of a minor ailment and go to a bar.

2 Rearrange a co-worker's desk very slightly so they won't be able to find anything.

3 Call a friend on another continent at the company's expense.

4 Draft resignation letter including random words from the dictionary such as "slattern" or "discombobulation."

5 Flirt with someone in accounts.

6 Fail to follow simple instructions to annoy the boss.

7 Online shopping hour.

8 Email friends.

Managers

1 Call meeting to delegate workload.

2 All afternoon lunch, get very drunk.

3 Fall asleep in motivation seminar.

4 Compose an all-staff email full of words like "interface" and "rationalization."

5 Obsequious hour, make the boss feel superior.

6 Review the trade press, internet, recruitment agencies for executive job openings.

7 Discipline a member of staff, just because.

8 Organize team building session that no-one wants to attend.

Executives

1 Downsize staff in order to maximize profits and your own bonus.

2 Attend international conference with a young "assistant."

3 Impress on staff that you're "one of them" by visiting desks and patronizing them.

4 Upgrade company car / plane / yacht.

5 Cut staff benefits.

6 Visit "the club" to catch up on essential drinking and snoozing.

7 Raid worker's pension fund.

8 Sexually harrass an underling.

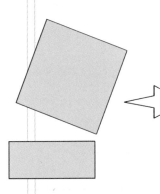 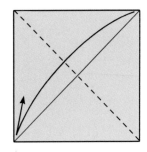

1   Begin with a large square cut from a sheet of photocopy size or US letter size paper.

2   Fold in half diagonally, crease firmly, then unfold.

3   Fold in half in the alternate direction, crease firmly, then unfold.

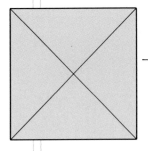 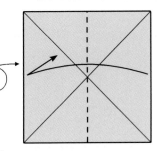 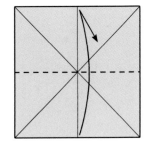

4   Turn over sideways.

5   Fold in half from right to left, crease firmly, then unfold.

6   Fold in half from bottom to top, crease firmly, then unfold.

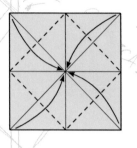

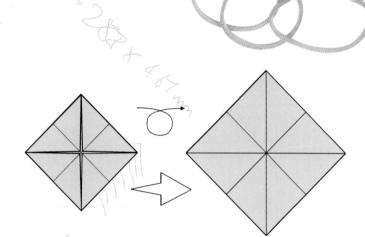

7 Fold all four corners to the center.

8 Turn over sideways. The next picture has been drawn to a larger scale.

9 The square is divided into eight triangles by the creases you have made. Mark each of the triangles with a number corresponding to one of the pre-selected decisions in your list.

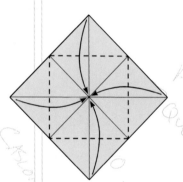

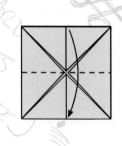

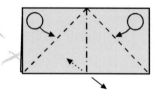

10 Once you have added the numbers fold all four corners to the center to hide them from view.

11 Fold in half from top to bottom. The next picture has been drawn to a larger scale.

12 Take hold of one side of the paper in each hand (at the points marked with circles) then swivel your hands toward each other, allowing the bottom center of the paper to open. The result will look like picture 13.

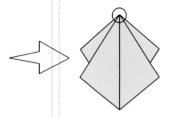

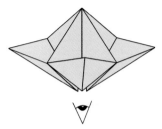

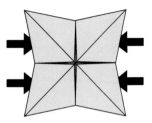

13 There are four pockets at the point marked with a circle. Open out each of these pockets in turn.

14 This is the traditional paperfold known as the Saltcellar. The next picture is drawn from the viewpoint shown.

15 This picture shows the design from above. Insert the thumb and first finger of your left hand into the pockets on the left hand side and the thumb and first finger of your right hand into the pockets on the right hand side.

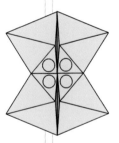

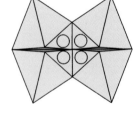

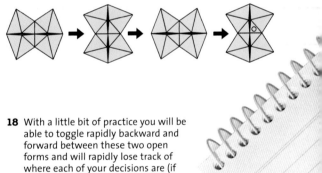

16 By keeping your hands close together but moving your thumbs and fingers apart you can make the center of the design open like this. The flaps marked with circles conceal four of your decisions.

17 By keeping moving your thumbs and fingers together but moving your hands slightly apart you can make the center of the design open like this. The flaps marked with circles conceal your other four decisions.

18 With a little bit of practice you will be able to toggle rapidly backward and forward between these two open forms and will rapidly lose track of where each of your decisions are (if you ever knew). Stop any time you like, choose one of the flaps at random, open it out and ... hey presto! ... your decision has been made.

Elephant on a Motorbike

Elephant on a Motorbike is a simple paperfold that offers ample opportunity for insulting people. For full effect try it on a manager at the end of a performance review, just after they've done the "pulling together as a team" bit. Everyone will already be secretly hating them and they won't be able to afford to take offense and not look like one of the boys when everyone is laughing. Depending on how much you dislike the victim you can substitute the word "elephant" for others like "idiot," "dork," and many more that are really great, but unfortunately unsuitable to print. The victim needs to be sitting down at the time. Choose someone who you know is thoroughly loathed.

It works like this. First fold a strip of paper into the simple apparatus shown in picture 7, then ask your unsuspecting victim what they think it is a model of. When they admit defeat say, "I'll show you." Persuade them to hold the bottom of the "V" firmly between their knees and to take hold of one of the arms of the apparatus in each hand. Now get them to hunch forward and make a low but loud humming noise. They will have no idea what is going on. Keep this going for a while, encouraging them to make louder and louder humming noises, then say, "It's an Elephant on a Motorbike." Your victim will be forced to laugh as loudly as anyone or look like a miserable killjoy. (OK, it ain't Woody Allen, but what do you expect at these prices?)

Origin: Unknown. Adaptation of a traditional sucker effect.

What to use: A long strip of paper cut from an photocopy size or US letter size sheet.

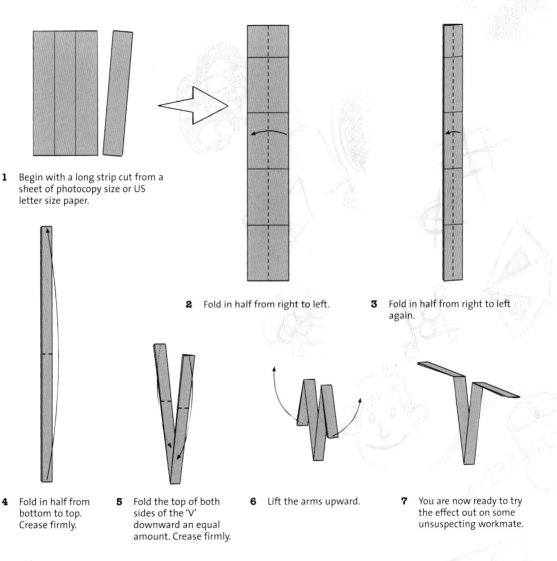

1 Begin with a long strip cut from a sheet of photocopy size or US letter size paper.

2 Fold in half from right to left.

3 Fold in half from right to left again.

4 Fold in half from bottom to top. Crease firmly.

5 Fold the top of both sides of the 'V' downward an equal amount. Crease firmly.

6 Lift the arms upward.

7 You are now ready to try the effect out on some unsuspecting workmate.

Easy Glider

Paper planes can provide a useful backup system for those not infrequent occasions when your company's IT systems go down. This glider is perfect for the task, with a wingspan that will keep it aloft across most office spaces, and good accuracy. It's not 100% reliable but then neither is email.

To send your "p-mail" you'll need to remember how to write in longhand. Don't panic—after a few practice attempts it will all come flooding back to you (the trick is in holding the pencil properly). Simply write your message on a sheet of paper, fold into a suitable plane-shaped packet, then launch in the general direction of the intended recipient. If you message fails to reach its correct destination immediately, other members of staff will probably be more than happy to act as airnet p-mail servers and redirect it for you.

It's useful to remember that like email, p-mail can be intercepted and read by others, so it's best not used for declarations of love or salacious gossip. However, if you can forge co-worker's handwriting you might want to pen a few aircraft that mock the boss's sexual prowess. It's amazing how easily navigation equipment can fail in even the most sophisticated designs . . .

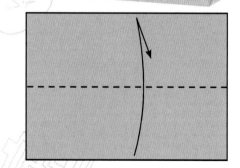

Origin: Designed by David Mitchell.

What to use: Easy Glider can be made from any sheet of photocopy size or US letter size paper.

1 Fold in half from bottom to top, crease firmly, then unfold. (If you are making your Easy Glider from the front of a used envelope the stamp should be in the top right hand corner here).

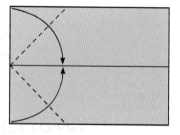

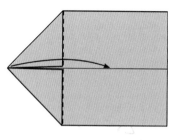

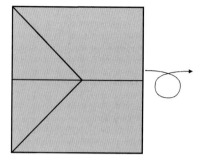

2 Fold both left hand corners inward using the horizontal center crease as a guide.

3 Fold the left hand point across to the right using the edges of the triangular flaps as a guide.

4 This is the result. Turn over sideways.

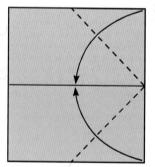

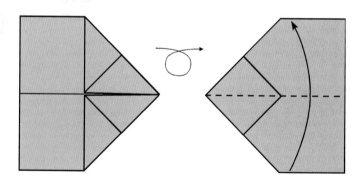

5 Fold both right hand corners inward using the horizontal center crease as a guide.

6 Turn over sideways again.

7 Fold in half from bottom to top. Crease firmly.

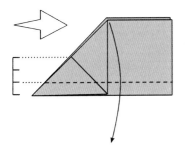

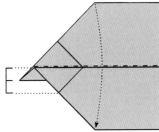

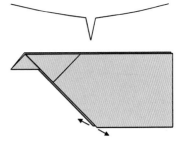

8 Fold the front wing downward in the way shown here. Try to make sure the new crease lies parallel to the bottom edge.

9 Fold the other wing down behind so that the edges of the wings line up exactly. Crease firmly.

10 Open up the wings to match this profile. (It is easier to see the profile if you view the wings from behind the tail.)

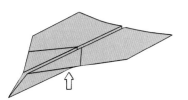

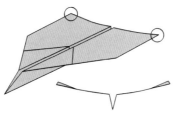

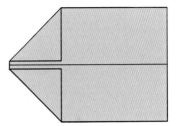

11 The Easy Glider is finished. Hold here to launch with a gentle forward push.

12 The Easy Glider should float gently away from you in a straight line losing height very slowly. If your glider loses height too quickly you can correct this by curling the back corners of the wings (marked with circles on the picture) gently upward to match the profile shown. If the glider veers to one side you need to gently adjust the angle (or curl) of the wings to balance the profile. Very small adjustments can have big effects.

13 You may also like to experiment with varying fold 2. Not folding the edges all the way onto the center line will result in larger wings and less weight up front. Both of these changes will affect the glide angle. Depending on the exact change that you make the Easy Glider may fly farther or it may stall more easily. You can also vary the folds made in steps 5, 8, and 9 to good (or bad) effect. Somewhere in there is the perfect paper plane.

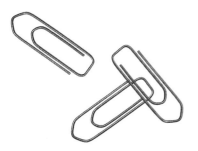

Jet Fighter

The Jet Fighter is a very different kind of paper plane: a state-of-the-art attack unit complete with powered take off and enhanced stinger nose casing. Like any powerful weaponry it should be used judiciously and only in times of great need. In extremis though, it is good to know you have some serious firepower in your corner.

Most paper planes are thrown by hand but the Jet Fighter is launched using a rubber band, which gives it accuracy, distance, and power. Nothing will wreck an adversary's concentration like a Jet Fighter to the side of the head. Within seconds all out war will ensue. A war in which you will prevail, for the Jet Fighter is superior to any other paper missile yet developed. (The Delta wings and canard foreplanes no doubt remind you of the Eurofighter Typhoon.) If you quietly stockpile a squadron of these before commencing an attack your air supremacy is assured. In the words of Donald Rumsfeld, we are not looking for air superiority here, but air dominance. You can trim the Jet Fighter for flight indoors, but because of the rubber band powered boost its full potential can perhaps best be seen when launched from a tall building, such as—say—any corporate headquarters. Indeed, there are few martial sights more stirring than an entire department lined up against the windows launching a flurry of Jet Fighters down upon a hapless manager.

Try to choose a calm, almost windless day, and then unleash hell.

Origin: Designed by David Mitchell.

What to use: The Jet Fighter can be made from any reasonably thin sheet of photocopy size or US letter size paper. Scrap paper is ideal. You will also need a rubber band and a stapler.

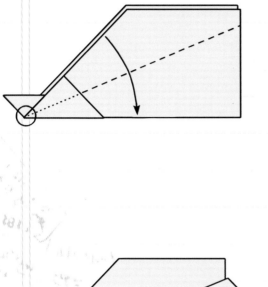

Begin by following steps 1 through 9 of the Easy Glider then arrange the paper in the way shown in picture 10 here.

10 Fold the sloping edge of the front wing downward to lie along the bottom edge. Look at picture 11 to see what the result should look like. You should only be folding the layers of the wing itself and not the pocket it runs into on the left. Make sure that the crease runs all the way to the point marked with a circle. You will find it easier to do this if you open up the pocket slightly while you make the fold.

11 This is the result. Turn over sideways.

12 Repeat step 10 on the other wing.

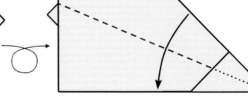

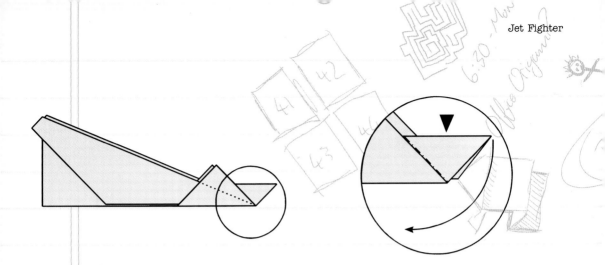

13 Follow the instructions in the enlargements to form the nose into a hook.

14 Turn the tip of the nose inside out between the layers of the fuselage. Crease firmly.

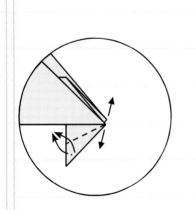

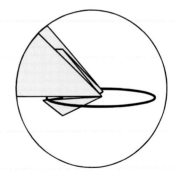

15 Open the nose and turn the tip of the triangular point inside out outside the other layers to form the hook.

16 Make sure there is a small gap between the hook and the underside of the fuselage into which a thin rubber band can be slipped.

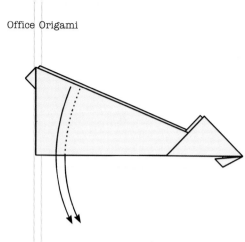

17 Fold the wings downward in front and behind.

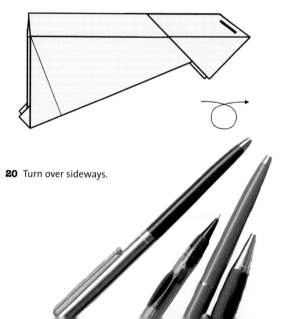

18 Put a staple through the nose to hold all the layers together.

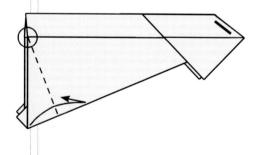

19 Make this small fold to form a control surface, crease firmly, then unfold.

20 Turn over sideways.

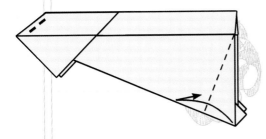

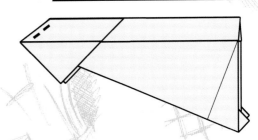

21 Repeat fold 19 on this wing as well.

22 Lift the wings up to match the profile shown.

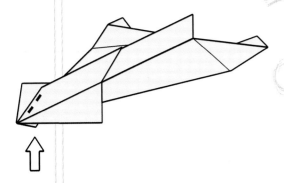

Tip: You can trim the Jet Fighter for flight indoors but because of the rubber band powered launch it is best to launch it for real outdoors in a wide open space. Try to choose a calm, almost windless day.

23 Hold the Jet Fighter by the hook and test launch gently forward. If the control surfaces are trimmed correctly the plane will glide at a shallow angle in the fuselage up position. Adjust the control surfaces until this has been achieved.

24 To launch the Jet Fighter first slip a long thin rubber band onto the hook. Loop the band onto the tip of your thumb, hold the back of the fuselage in your other hand and pull back to tension the band. Release the plane upward at a sharp angle. It will catapult into the air, perhaps loop the loop (depending on how the control surfaces have been trimmed) and glide away in the least expected direction.

Towers of Tokyo

The Towers of Tokyo shimmering, beautiful in the afternoon sunlight, all is tranquil. People rush to work through the city's busy streets or relax in its parks, little aware of the horror that faces them. What's this? A giant monster, breathing fire and with laser beams shooting out of its eyes descends on the peaceful city and tears it to rubble. Nothing can stop the rampaging creature, its fury levels all before it. People are trampled beneath its feet as building after building is torn asunder.

This project offers the ultimate in stress relief and anger management. The ethos is simple, you construct a city around and on your desk and—subject to office layout—encroaching on other people's desks. These towers are easy to construct and rather elegant. Your co-workers will watch in wonder as over days, weeks, months the metropolis grows before their eyes, mostly when you are on the phone and have nothing to do with your hands.

All is well in the city until you have a bad day—a deal doesn't happen, the boss is furious, and some idiot suggests you might want to tidy your desk. Before the quailing office Godzilla arises from your chair, and the Towers of Tokyo are doomed.

But there is hope. From the ashes a new city will arise, fearing the return of the creature but hoping that none will disturb its slumber. The creature itself rests, knowing that none will again be so foolish as to tell it to tidy its desk.

Origin: Design by David Mitchell.

What to use: The design will work from rectangular paper of any proportions, but photocopy or US letter size paper is ideal. You can make the tubes smaller by dividing your paper into halves or quarters before you begin. If you use squares all the tubes will be the same size and shape, but it will still be possible to use them to build.

Folding the long, thin tubes

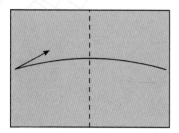

1 Fold in half from right to left, crease firmly, then unfold.

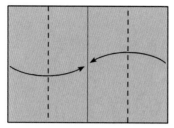

2 Fold the right and left edges inwards to lie along the vertical center crease.

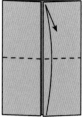

3 Fold in half from bottom to top, crease firmly, then unfold.

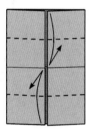

4 Fold the top and bottom edges inward to lie along the horizontal center crease, crease firmly, then unfold.

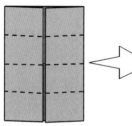

5 Use the creases made in steps 3 and 4 to roll the paper into the shape shown in picture 6.

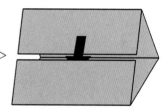

6 Begin to form the tube by inserting one end of the paper inside the other.

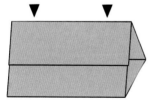

7 Lay the partly formed tube on a flat surface and apply gentle, even pressure on the top edge to persuade the two ends to slide completely inside each other.

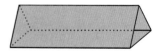

8 The first long tube is finished. When building pagodas, long tubes are always used in pairs.

Folding the short, fat tubes

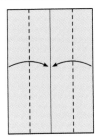

1 Fold in half from right to left, crease firmly, then unfold.

2 Fold the right and left hand edges inward to lie along the vertical center crease.

3 Fold in half from top to bottom, crease firmly, then unfold.

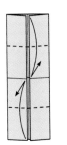

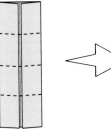

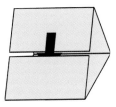

4 Fold the top and bottom edges inward to lie along the horizontal center crease, crease firmly, then unfold.

5 Use the creases made in steps 3 and 4 to roll the paper into the form shown in picture 6.

6 Begin forming the tube by inserting one end of the paper inside the other.

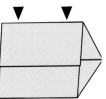

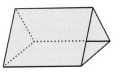

7 Lay the partly formed tube on a flat surface like this and apply gentle, even pressure to the top edge to persuade the flaps to slide completely inside each other.

8 The first short tube is finished. When building pagodas, short tubes are also always used in pairs.

Building the towers

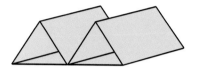

1   Arrange two short tubes side by side.

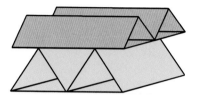

2   Then lay two long tubes across them so that the edges of the layers are aligned vertically.

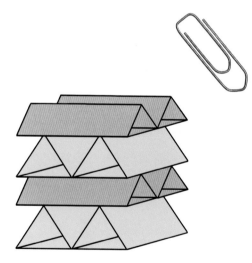

3   Add alternate layers of short and long tubes to build up the layers of the tower.

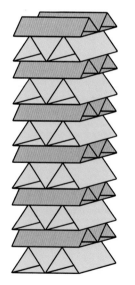

4   The first Toppling Tower is finished. This one is easy.

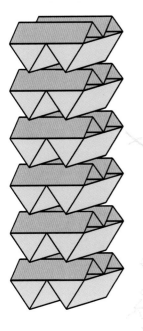

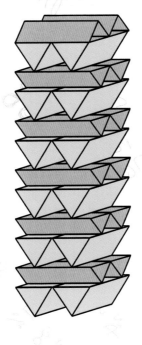

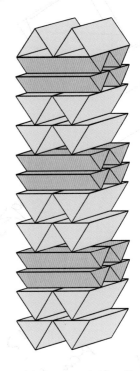

5 This one is more difficult.

6 This one is more difficult still (especially for just one person).

7 And this one is probably quite impossible.

Hippy Suncatcher

The corporate environment can be quite, well, corporate. For some reason the business tycoons tend to nix friendly interior design during planning conversations with architects and designers. Sleek lines, gunmetal grey, chrome, and black leather is all very well, but it means that the room might lack the kind of far out, psychedelic chutzpah that can transform an office into the kind of pad where you can just trip out on the vibe. Fortunately, this can soon be remedied with just a few sticky notes. You'll be amazed at how quickly spartan Philippe Starck, I. M. Pei, or Le Corbusier interiors can be brightened up. Start with your own area and soon everyone will be following your lead. The office as you know it will be invisible beneath a sea of slowly fading, curling sticky notes.

This Suncatcher is made from square message notes that are attached to a window by their sticky strips. Because message notes are translucent, overlapping them in geometric patterns produces a groovy stain glass window effect. Seen against the light, those areas where the message notes overlap each other will show darker than those areas where they don't. The more layers, the darker the color. It'll really freak you out. All you need now is some sun to catch, so this project is not ideal if you happen to be reading this book in London.

Plus, of course, if you ever run out of sticky notes and need one in a real hurry, you'll know exactly where to find one.

What to use: Square message notes. Some notes, and some colors, are more translucent than others. Smaller notes work better than large ones.

Origin: Concept and design by David Mitchell.

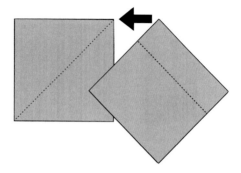

1 Begin by attaching your first message note to the middle of a window by the sticky strip. Make sure the sides of the note are vertical. The position of the sticky strip is indicated by the dotted line. You will get a better result if you remove the notes from the pad without allowing them to curl.

2 Lay a second note onto the first so that the edge of the second note lies along the diagonal of the first. Note the position of the sticky strip on the second note. All the sticky strips of all the notes should lie around the outer edge of the design.

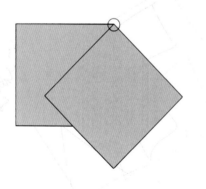

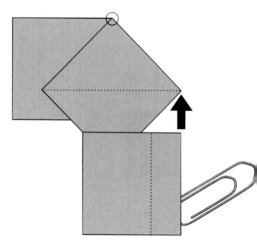

3 Make sure the corners of the two notes lie exactly on top of each other, and that the sloping edge of the second note points directly at the lower left hand corner of the first.

4 Continue to add notes in the same way until your Suncatcher is complete.

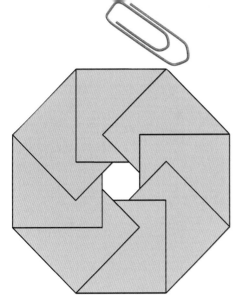

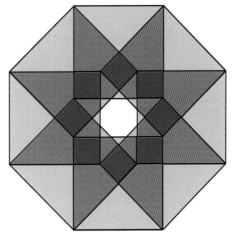

5 This is the result. You will see that the last note has been tucked underneath the first note to complete the pattern.

6 Because message notes are slightly translucent your Suncatcher should now look like this.

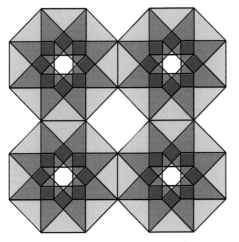

7 You can combine several Suncatchers into a larger pattern. You may also like to find out for yourself what happens if you make Suncatchers from notes of two or more different colors. It's definitely worth trying!

The Cling-On Cube

Oᴋ, so at first sight this is not the most inspiring project in the book. But give it a try, you'll find it's addictive and, like all good Office Origami, the more time-consuming and absorbing it is the less time you'll have for doing all those annoying little things for which you receive what they laughably call your "salary." The basic cube is unimpressive; folded and assembled from business cards or 3 x 5" index cards. However, like the plastic bricks you played with as a child the only limits of the Cling-on Cube are your imagination. Those little flaps sticking out mean that they can be locked together to form bigger objects. Much bigger objects. So, tell whoever orders the business cards that the entire department needs three-year supplies and get to work. Here are some ideas:

• Your own signage to hang over your desk, reading "Harry's Bar."

• Detailed model of Notre Dame Cathedral, built to scale.

• Exact recreation of the space under the stairs where Mommy put you when you were very, very bad.

• A model of your boss that night when you were both really drunk and which is never again to be referred to.

• An assistant named Pierre who will accompany you to take notes at all future meetings.

Origin: The design is traditional in Europe and The USA. In its original form the cube was made from six playing cards.

What to use: Business cards or 3 x 5" file cards, or, of course, playing cards, if you happen to work for a manufacturer or in Las Vegas.

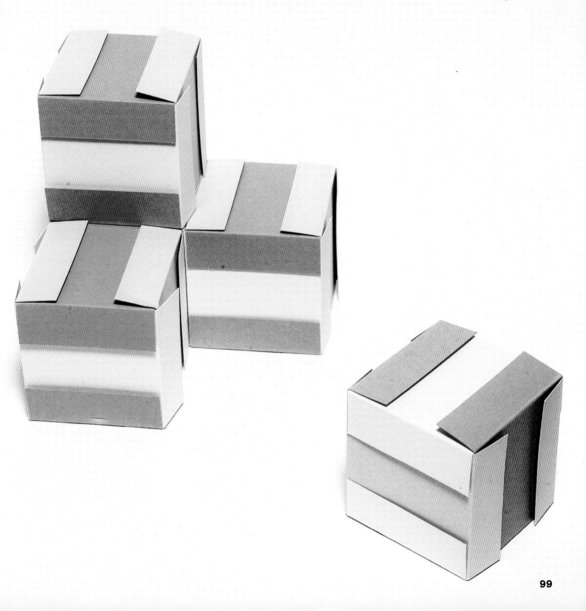

Folding the modules

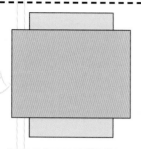

1 Arrange two cards like this so that the surfaces you want to show on the outside of the cube are touching each other face to face. Try to make sure that the cards are centered evenly.

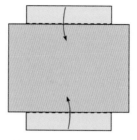

2 Fold the ends of the rear card tightly around the edges of the front card and crease firmly.

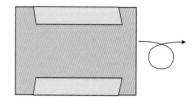

3 This is the result. Turn over sideways.

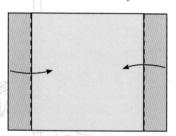

4 Fold the ends of the rear card tightly around the edges of the front card and crease firmly.

5 The cards should now be firmly locked together. Take them apart taking care to open out the folds as little as possible. (In the assembly diagrams many of the flaps have been shown in a slightly splayed position. This is to help make the pictures clear. You will get a better looking cube if you keep enough spring in the folds to hold the flaps tight against the faces of the cube.)

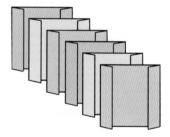

6 Repeat steps 1 through 5 on the other two pairs of cards.

Assembling the cube

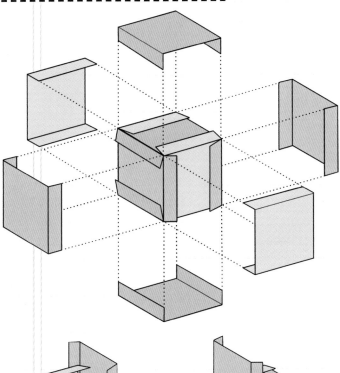

7 This picture provides an overview of how the 6 cards go together. Note that all the flaps go outside the other cards. Pictures 8 through 12 take you through the assembly process in detail, card by card.

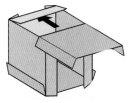

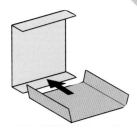

8 The first two cards slide together like this.

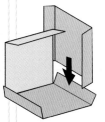

9 Add the third card of the third color.

10 The fourth card goes in like this.

11 And the fifth like this.

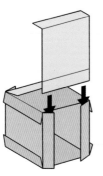

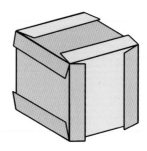

12 Slide the sixth card into place to complete the cube.

13 The Cling-On Cube is finished.

Building cubes into lattices

Pictures 14 through 17 show you how to build a second cube on top of the first. If you have enough cards and enough patience you can continue this process to create large lattices of integrated Cling-On Cubes in this way.

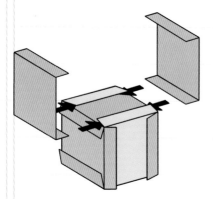

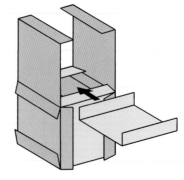

14 Add two more cards underneath the flaps of the existing cube.

15 Slide the third card into position.

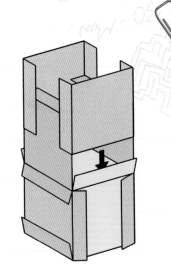

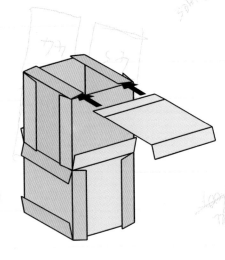

16 Add two more cards like this.

17 Slide the last card into place to complete the second cube.

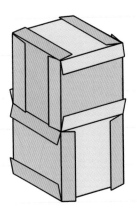

18 Two cubes have been joined together. Further cubes can be added to any face in a similar way.

19 The only limit to the size of the structures you can create is the number of suitable cards you have available.

The Multimodule

The Multimodule forms the basis of some serious Office Origami. This is the level you attempt only if you are an international criminal mastermind, with a white cat on your knees and a shark pit round the back. Your co-workers will now begin to look at you with fear in their eyes and you will begin to find that they tremble before you. This is a great time to start building your own private army. Best of all though, this is another sticky note project, and as any regular stationery store user knows, sticky notes breed during the night. There is an inexhaustible supply of them.

This project shows you how to fold the Multimodule from 3 x 5" message notes and how to configure and assemble six modules to make a very attractive and stable cube, just right for toying with, idly, as you give orders for an inferior to be thrown to the sharks. The next project shows you how the same module can be used to build Multimodule Stars.

Origin: The Multimodule is a development of the classic Sonobe module (named after its inventor, the Japanese paperfolder Mitsonobu Sonobe), which is folded from a square.

What to use: 3 x 5" message notes. You will need one message note for each module. You need six modules to make a cube. An attractive effect can be obtained by using two notes in each of three contrasting but complementary colors, a quiet word with whoever orders the stationery and possibly a few pastries will assure you of these, but you can also fold Multimodules from photocopy size or US letter size paper.

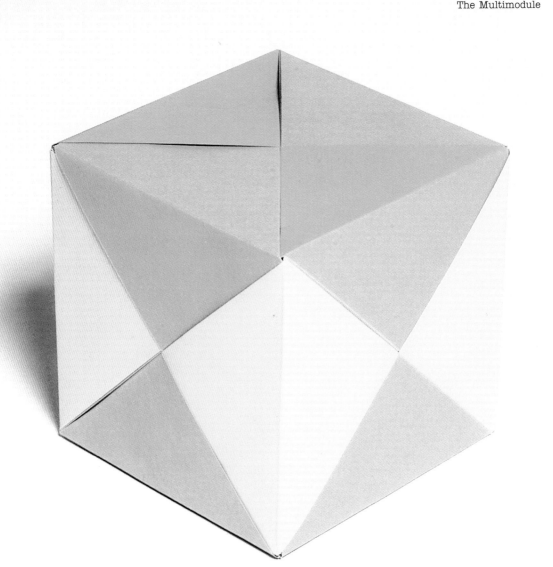

Folding the Multimodule

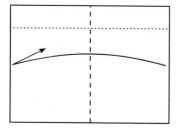

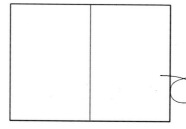

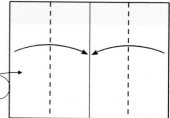

1 The position of the sticky strip is shown by the dotted line. It should not be visible. Fold in half from right to left, crease firmly, then unfold.

2 Turn over sideways.

3 Fold both right and left hand edges inward to lie along the vertical crease made in step 1.

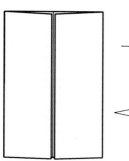

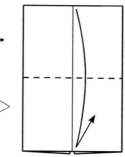

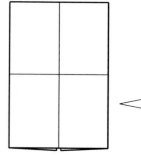

4 Turn over sideways.

5 Fold in half from top to bottom, crease firmly, then unfold.

6 Turn over sideways. The next picture has been drawn to a larger scale.

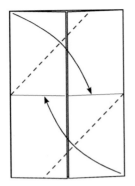

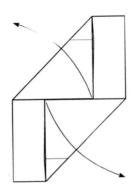

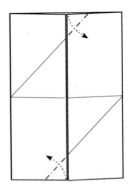

7 Fold the top left and bottom right hand corners inward so that the edges butt against each other along the line of the horizontal crease made in step 5.

8 Open out the folds you made in step 7.

9 Fold these two small triangular flaps away inside the layers of the module by reversing the creases made in step 8.

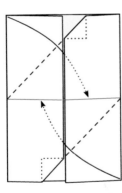

11 This is the result. The base form of the Multimodule is finished. Each module has two flaps and two pockets which can be used to link the modules together. Six modules can be used to make a cube.

10 Remake the folds made in step 8 but this time tuck the corners in between the layers of the module in the way shown.

Configuring the Multimodule to make a cube

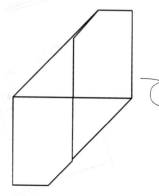

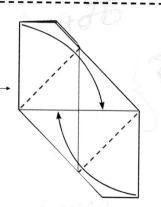

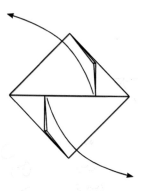

12 Turn the module over sideways.

13 Fold the top left and bottom right hand corners inward so that the edges butt against each other along the line of the horizontal crease made in step 5.

14 Raise both flaps at right angles.

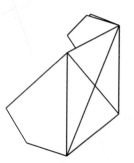

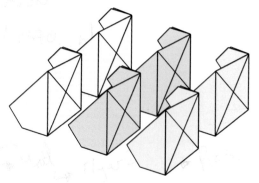

15 The Multimodule has been configured for the cube. The result should look like this. Fold and configure all six modules.

16 For an attractive result use two modules in each of three contrasting but complementary colors.

Assembling the Multimodule cube

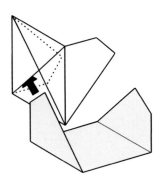

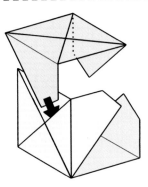

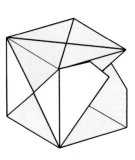

17 The first two modules go together like this.

18 Add the third in a similar way.

19 One face of the cube has been completed.

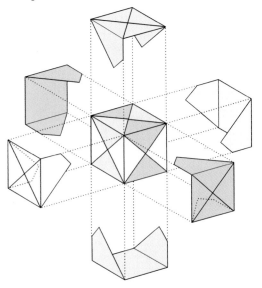

20 This picture provides an overview of the way in which the cube is assembled. Multimodules of the same color form opposite faces. Each face is made up of part of three adjacent modules that go together in the way shown in pictures 17 through 19. Continue adding modules in the same way using the pattern of colors shown here until all six faces are complete.

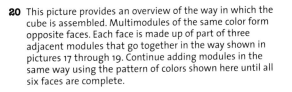

21 The Multimodule Cube is finished.

Multimodule Stars

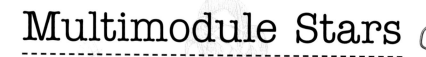

This is not origami to be tossed lightly aside, this is origami to be left at the scene of a crime, beside the body or the broken jewel cabinet as a symbol of your sticky note prowess and your defiance of authority. In an office environment you should aim to build it nonchalantly during meetings as part of a takeover attempt, peeling off the sticky notes without looking and building the Star as you speak languidly about your plans to crush continents, your competitors, and the photocopier service contractor beneath your heel. If it goes right you will look cool beyond measure. Fold this perfectly without once looking at it and you will be in complete control of the company by the end of the meeting.

Of course, if it all goes wrong and you're left desperately trying to fix a droopy pile of non-sticky sticky notes you will look more foolish than anyone in the history of the world and may as well shuffle out of the special small door that every company has for losers and has-beens. So, as you can see it is important to be sure of your ability before you begin.

Perfecting Multimodule Stars will keep you occupied for hours. And even the practice attempts will have benefits— you'll be receiving loyalty gifts from all the major sticky note manufacturers. You may also notice that your productivity drops to record lows.

Origin: See page 104.

What to use: 3 x 5" message notes. You will need one message note for each module. You need twelve modules (three in each of four colors) to make a small star and thirty modules (five in each of six colors) to make a large one. You can also fold Multimodules from photocopy size or US letter size paper.

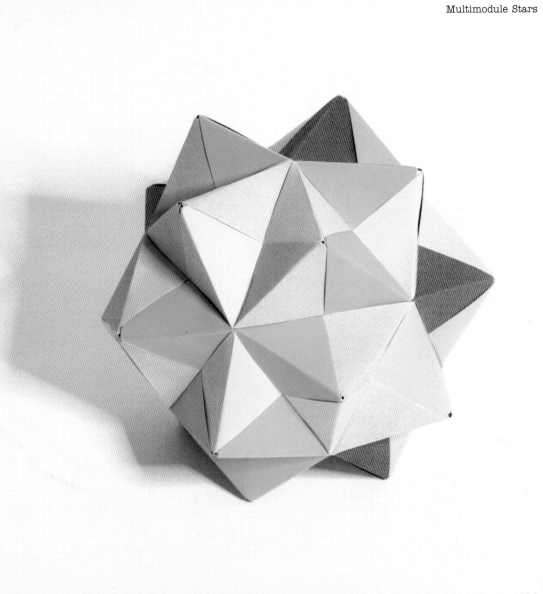

Configuring the Multimodule

The Multimodule is configured in the same way for both stars.

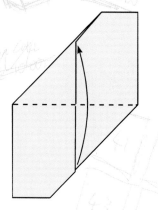

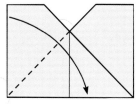

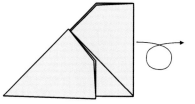

1 Fold the module in half from bottom to top.

2 Fold the left hand edge onto the bottom edge.

3 Turn over sideways.

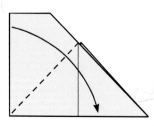

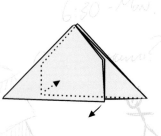

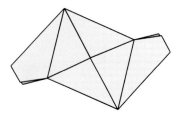

4 Repeat step 2 on the other half of the paper.

5 Open out the front and back flaps so that the module looks like picture 6.

6 The process of configuring the Multimodule to make the Multimodule Stars is finished.

Making the Small Multimodule Star

You will need twelve sheets of paper altogether. An attractive effect can be obtained by using three sheets in each of four contrasting but complementary colors. Fold all the sheets into Multimodules and configure them in the way shown in steps 1 through 6. The star is built out of eight three-sided pyramids. Before you begin to assemble the whole star it is a good idea to practice making one of these pyramids all by itself. Picture 7 shows you how to do this.

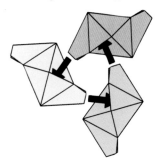

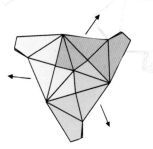

7 Three modules go together to form a pyramid like this.

8 In this picture the top of the pyramid is pointing towards you. The top of the pyramids form the blunt points of the star. Once you are confident you have made this pyramid correctly take it apart again.

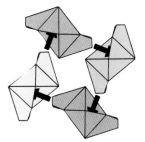

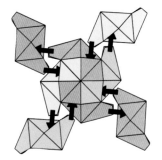

9 Put the first four modules (one of each color) together like this. This assembly will lie flat but it will be easier to add the next four modules if you allow the modules to remain three-dimensional.

10 Add the next four modules (again one of each color) like this. As you add each module it will complete a three-sided pyramid. When you have finished adding all four modules you will have a ring of four pyramids. This ring will not lie flat. The center of the ring should be convex not concave.

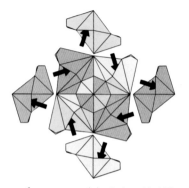

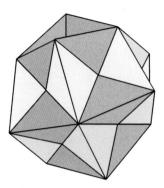

11 There are four more modules to be added. The picture shows where they go. As you add each module the star will begin to form. When you have finished you will have four loose flaps at the back. There is a pocket for each of these close by. Tuck them all in and the small Multimodule Star will be finished.

12 The finished star should look like this. If you have followed the instructions correctly each of the four colors should form a ring all the way around the star.

Making the Large Multimodule Star

You will need thirty sheets of paper altogether. An attractive effect can be obtained by using five sheets in each of six contrasting but complementary colors. Fold all the sheets into Multimodules and configure them in the way shown in steps 1 through 6. The large star is made in a similar way to the small one, but the larger number of modules involved means it is harder to assemble. It is a good idea to make the small star before you move on to tackle this one.

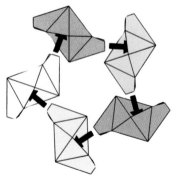

13 Put the first five modules (all of different colors) together like this. This assembly will not lie flat. The center of the assembly should be convex not concave.

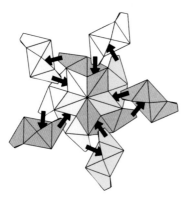

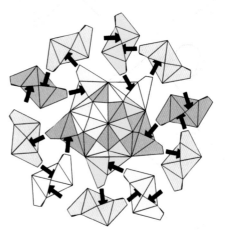

14 Add the next four modules (another one of each of the same five colors) like this. As you add each module it will complete a three-sided pyramid. When you have finished adding all five modules you will have a ring of five pyramids. This ring will not lie flat. The center of the ring should be convex not concave.

15 This picture shows you how to add the five modules of the sixth color and the next module of the existing five. When you have finished adding all these modules you will have created a second ring of five pyramids surrounding the first five. By this stage the pattern of the colors and the way in which the modules go together is well established and you will find it quite easy to add the remaining modules in a similar way.

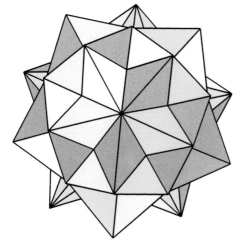

16 The finished star should look like this. Each of the six colors should form a ring all the way around the star.

The Magic Tube

Tired of being plain old Joe or Jane from Sales and Marketing? Now, with Office Origami and the wave of a wand you can become Mysterioso, Sub-Assistant Sales Executive of the Dark Arts. Cape, twirly moustache, and sparkly leotard-clad assistant are optional, but can be easily made with scrap paper by the adept Office Origamist.

This ingenious device will keep you amused for at least an afternoon or two and will also puzzle and amaze your co-workers. At times, a short, fat tube and, at other times, a tall thin one, only you can switch smoothly between the two. The entrepreneurial type will easily find a way of winning drinks in the bar after work with it.

What to use: The instructions show you how to make the Two-Way Tube from message notes but you can just as easily make it from two sheets of photocopy size or US letter size paper or virtually anything else. The exact proportions of the rectangles you begin with are not crucial (although if you use squares you will find that both tubes are exactly the same size). In these instructions the message note used to make each of the modules has been shaded a different color. This is to help you see what has to be done more clearly, but when you make your own Two-Way Tube you will get a more magical effect if both modules are the same color.

Origin: The original Two-Way Tube was invented by the American magician Robert E. Neale and was made from a single piece of card. This two-part version was designed by David Mitchell.

116

Folding module 1

If you are using message notes the note should be arranged so that the sticky strip is behind the paper on the right hand side.

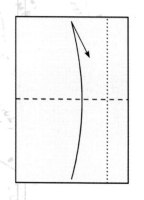

1 Fold in half from bottom to top, crease firmly, then unfold.

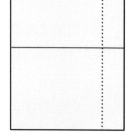

2 Turn over sideways.

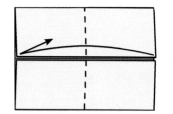

4 Fold in half from right to left, crease firmly, then unfold.

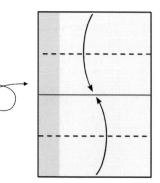

3 Fold the top and bottom edges inward to lie along the horizontal center crease you made in step 1.

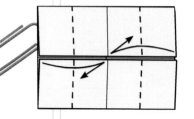

5 Fold the left and right hand edges inward to lie along the vertical center crease, crease firmly, then unfold.

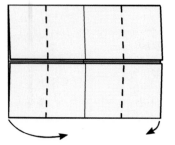

6 Swing the right and left hand flaps forward at right angles.

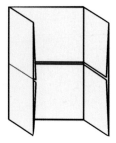

7 Module 1 is finished.

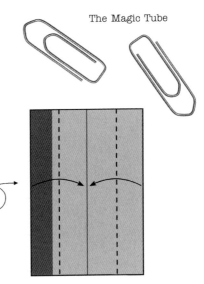

Folding module 2

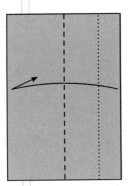

8 Fold in half from right to left, crease firmly, then unfold.

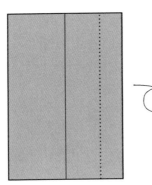

9 Turn over sideways.

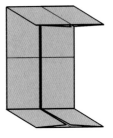

10 Fold the right and left hand edges inward to lie along the vertical center crease.

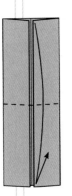

11 Fold in half from top to bottom, crease firmly, then unfold.

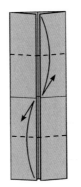

12 Fold the top and bottom edges inward to lie along the horizontal center crease.

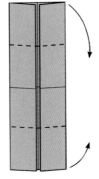

13 Swing the top and bottom flaps forward at right angles.

14 Module 2 is finished.

Assembling the modules

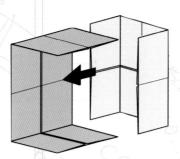

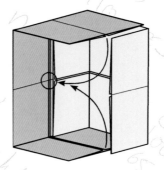

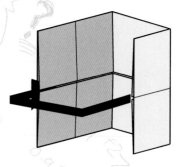

15 Slide the left hand flap of module 1 inside the right hand end of module 2 like this.

16 Fold the top flap down and the bottom flap up to lock module 1 in place. The centers of the end of both flaps end up at the point marked with a circle.

17 Slide the right hand flap of module 1 inside the left hand end of module 2 in a similar way. This looks difficult but is quite easy to do in practice.

Locating the tubes

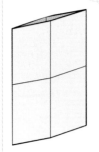

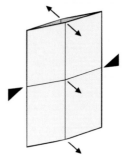

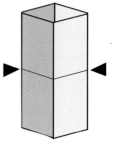

18 This is the result. The modules are assembled.

19 Open like this to find the tall, thin tube.

20 This is the tall, thin tube. Squash flat again like this to begin to change to the short, fat tube.

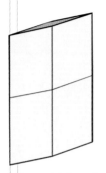

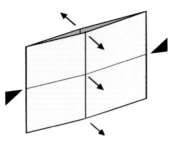

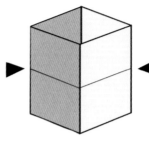

21 Rotate the model through 90 degrees so that it looks like picture 22.

22 Open like this to find the short, fat tube.

23 This is the short, fat tube.

Presenting the Magic Tube

The Magic Tube can be enjoyed as a paradoxical object in its own right or presented as a magic trick.

To perform the trick for your friends you will need two Magic Tubes of different colors, say blue and mauve, and an envelope into which they will fit when folded flat. Arrange the mauve one as a tall, thin tube and the blue one as a short, fat tube.

Have the envelope examined by a friend before you start. It's always good to demonstrate that the ordinary things you use in magic tricks are just that—ordinary. Begin by showing that the mauve tube will pass right through the blue tube.

Now challenge one of your friends to remember which tube goes through which. Easy, right?

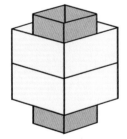

Flatten the tubes, put them in the envelope, seal it, rip it open, then take them out again. This time show that the blue tube will pass through the mauve tube. Memory is such an untrustworthy thing.

The envelope can, of course, be shown to be completely empty.

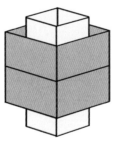

Repeat as many times as you like. This simple trick can be completely baffling to someone who has never seen the Magic Tube before.

The effect works best if you can pick the tubes out of the envelope and open them smoothly to the correct shape without any fumbling or hesitation. Practice makes perfect here, of course!

The Gift Box

It is an unfortunate, but inevitable part of today's office *mores* that you will at some point be expected to buy gifts for other workers. What with birthdays, leaving gifts, Secretary Day, or the dreaded Secret Santa, it will seem like someone in the office has got their hand out almost every day.

The Gift Box works on the same principle as the Frog Eat Frog card. From henceforth you will simply refuse to contribute to any collection, as you'd "rather give dear Mary something a little more personal." Five minutes later, a beautiful presentation box that they can keep staples in. Or pins, or whatever. If you're feeling particularly generous you might even want to pre-fill it with the debris from the bottom of your desk drawer.

Mary won't be touched, but she'll have to say she is, which is just as good. It's worth remembering that your success here hangs on your ability to hand this over with sincerity. At the slightest suggestion

that you didn't actually make this out of the goodness of your heart and your number's up, so hand it over with a warm smile and a few words along the lines of "I know how important a tidy desk is to you, so I made you this." You might want to add, "I was going to buy something, but I thought you'd rather have a gift that would remind you of me." This means that poor Mary won't even be able to throw it away when you're not looking.

In the unlikely event that you actually like the person, don't forget that the perfect gift is a copy of *Office Origami*. And spreading the word is good for your karma too.

Origin: Designed by David Mitchell.

What to use: Square telephone pad paper is ideal, though you can fold the Stingy Santa Gift Box from any other kind of square paper as well. The larger the paper, the larger the box.

Folding The Gift Box

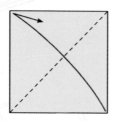

1 Fold in half diagonally, crease firmly, then unfold.

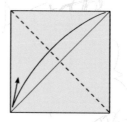

2 Fold in half in the alternate direction, crease firmly, then unfold.

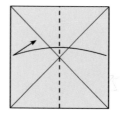

3 Fold in half from right to left, crease firmly, then unfold.

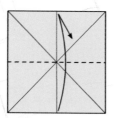

4 Fold in half from bottom to top, crease firmly, then unfold.

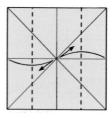

5 Fold the right and left hand edges inward to lie along the vertical center crease, crease firmly, then unfold.

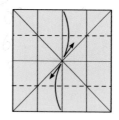

6 Fold the top and bottom edges inward to lie along the horizontal center crease, crease firmly, then unfold.

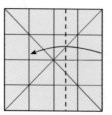

7 Fold the right hand edge across to lie along the vertical crease nearest to the left hand edge. Crease firmly.

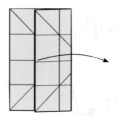

8 Unfold.

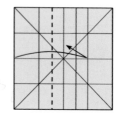

9 Fold the left hand edge across to lie along the vertical crease nearest to the right hand edge, crease firmly, then unfold.

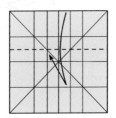

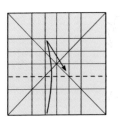

10 Fold the top edge downward to lie along the horizontal crease nearest to the bottom edge, crease firmly then unfold.

11 Fold the bottom edge upward to lie along the horizontal crease nearest to the top edge, crease firmly then unfold.

12 Check that you have made all the creases shown here. Turn over sideways.

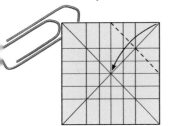

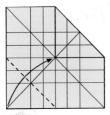

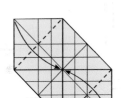

13 Fold the top right hand corner into the center.

14 Fold the bottom left hand corner into the center in a similar way.

15 Fold the remaining corners into the center as well.

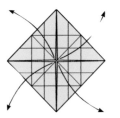

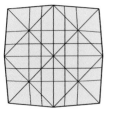

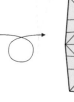

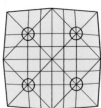

16 Open out the folds made in steps 13 through 15. Try to avoid flattening the creases as you do this.

17 Check that you have made all the creases shown here. Turn over sideways.

18 When you first turn the paper over the four corners will be pointing slightly away from you. Gently flip each corner forward in turn so that the points identified by circles become concave.

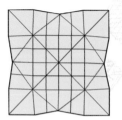

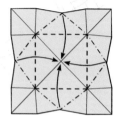

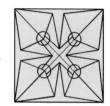

19 The result is a form like a shallow dish. For the sake of clarity the creases made is steps 7 through 11 will not be shown in pictures 20 through 30.

20 Fold the middle of each side into the centre of the dish using the existing creases.

21 Flatten the folds completely so that all the points marked with circles end up in the centre.

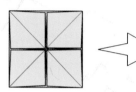

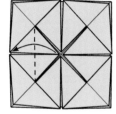

22 This is the result. The next picture has been drawn to a larger scale.

23 Fold all four front flaps in half outwards.

24 There are four flaps in the centre. Fold the point of the left hand flap outwards to the left hand edge as shown. Crease firmly.

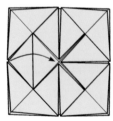

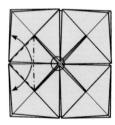

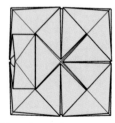

25 Unfold.

26 Make these folds simultaneously, by reversing the direction of the creases made in step 24. The point marked with a circle ends up at x.

27 This is the result. Repeat steps 24 through 26 on the other three flaps.

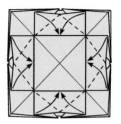

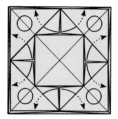

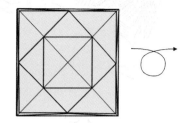

28 Your paper should now look like this. Fold all eight of the small triangular flaps inwards.

29 There is a pocket below each of the large flaps (identified by circles). Tuck the eight small triangular flaps into these pockets.

30 The result should look like this. Turn over sideways.

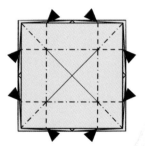

32 Insert two fingers inside the box to open up the layers then use the thumb and forefinger of the other hand to squeeze the corner into shape. Do this with each of the corners in turn. All the creases you need to form the box are already there. Some of the small triangular flaps may slip out of their pockets as you do this. Don't worry about this. It's quite simple to tuck them back in afterwards.

31 The base of the box is formed from the front layers by squeezing the sides of each corner together in turn. The central square, which forms the bottom of the box, rises up in front. Picture 32 shows you how to do this.

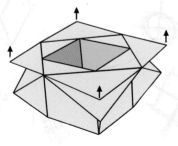

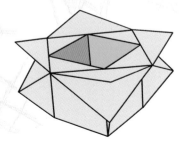

33 The result should look like this. Raise the top flaps slightly.

34 The Cute Container is finished.

Going Further with Origami

If the designs in this book have inspired you to fold you can learn more about origami by visiting
www.origamiheaven.com

For those who want to take things further still there are specialist origami clubs in many countries, which arrange meetings and publish magazines and collections of new designs. The two main English speaking clubs are the British Origami Society and Origami USA, both of which are

not-for-profit organizations run entirely by volunteers. Both clubs have a worldwide membership base.

Origami USA can be contacted through
www.origami-usa.org

The British Origami Society can be contacted through
www.britishorigami.org.uk